MW00577317

These
Haunted
Islands

Written by Chris Lake

Printed and bound by CPI Group (UK) Ltd, Croydon, CR0 4YY.

In Guernsey, when the accused had been found guilty,
the greffier (chief clerk) would draw little pictures of the
witch's fate in the margins of the court record books

ACKNOWLEDGEMENTS

My thanks (in no particular order) to:

Madeleine de la Haye; Pauline Syvret, Anna Baghiani and the staff at La Société
Jersiaise; the staff at the Central Library, St Helier; the Priaulx Library, Guernsey;
the Guille-Alles Library, Guernsey; the Salem Institute, Massachusetts; the Witch
Museum, Salem; the State Library of New Jersey, Trenton; the Rev. Robert Law;
Miss S. C. Greenwood; the Rev. Richard Shaw; the staff at the JEP and the Guernsey
Press; the Greffiers of both Guernsey and Jersey; Marion G. Turk; Ward Rutherford;
Helen Young; Mrs Nancy Maletroit; Sandra Harris and the Library at Highlands
College, Jersey; Laurie Cabot; and to G. R. Balleine for writing in such clear prose.
I must also thank Gary Grimshaw, Reg Cridland, Barbara Pitman, Wikipaedia, and
Carolyn Ainsworth for the pictures used in this book.

'Witchcraft in the Channel Islands' is dedicated to all members of 2L (as were) of
Les Quennevais School and Community Centre, Jersey, in 1976.

FOREWORD

'By the pricking of my thumbs,
Something wicked this way comes'.

Second Witch, Act IV, scene I (Macbeth)

'THESE Haunted Islands' looks at the history of witchcraft in a group of small offshore communities, the fear it was to spread throughout Britain and the Channel Islands and how just a few men pursued so-called witches with terrible fervour.

Without doubt some Islanders did turn to the Dark Side – usually in an effort to terrorise their neighbours – although a better name for Satanic practices is probably blackmail, for even in the 19th and 20th centuries Channel Islanders were known to play on the minds of others, sometimes frightening them so badly that they would pay anything to have a 'curse' removed.

In retrospect, it seems idiotic that the Devil would play mischievous tricks on people so that their crops wouldn't grow or their cattle would die when there were so many other greater evils which would certainly have been of far greater interest to Satan, including the Black Death or, in the 20th century, Stalin's purges which saw millions die ... but then Stalin and Communism had no use for religion, believing Christianity to be 'the Opium of the Masses'.

Be that as it may, what follows is a look at the witchcraft trials in the 16th and 17th centuries; commentary on how the Salem witch trials had Channel Island connections; one or two of the more apocryphal stories from the past plus a brief look at modern times, from Henrietta Lake in Guernsey and her use of the occult to frighten poor Mrs Houtin almost to death to 'The Beast of Jersey', Edward Paisnel, who probably hid behind the shield of Satan as justification for the crimes he was to commit for at least a decade.

After publication of 'These Haunted Islands' in 1986 I was upbraided for confusing witchcraft with Satanism yet I do recognise there is a huge difference between the two of them.

Over the years I have come to know four or five so-called

witches, each of whom assured me that they were no threat to God and that their every intent was meant to help cleanse the world, not destroy it.

As Rhianna Galvin, a practising Wicca, told the BBC recently: 'Witchcraft is goddess-based, and it's easier, it's kinder, it's gentler – there's no control, there's no guilt and there's no fear factor.'

Meanwhile in Salem, Laurie Cabot, the 'official' witch of Massachusetts, who maintains she is a direct descendant of the Cabots of Jersey, is allowed to officiate at weddings and also invites visitors to her website for a one in a million opportunity to join her 'every Thursday evening at 10 pm to psychically travel 700 feet straight up over Salem, (where) you will see a crystal wheel surrounding the entire parameter of the city of Salem.'

Having met Laurie, I can say that there is nothing frightening about her, although she can be quite unnerving, particularly when she tells you things about yourself or your family only you alone should know. If this sounds strange and out of date in an age of iPods and e-mails, consider this: Since 'These Haunted Islands' was published, for a period of ten years afterwards and on average twice a year I would be contacted by people wanting to know how to contact the Island exorcist.

One caller, for example, was from Alderney. His daughter, her father told me, was possessed.

Another woman who had recently left her boyfriend explained how he had cursed her and that since then, no matter how hard she tried and no matter how long she spent cleaning her flat, there was always a horrible smell in it – one that had never been there before the curse.

Meanwhile, it was only a year ago that I was contacted by an acquaintance who told me that first that the 'ghost' of an old woman, wearing a shawl and secondly that of a man had been seen in pubs in St Helier. The woman allegedly said to startled visitors: 'Help me – my husband's trying to kill me!' The hotel's bar 'loo', where the woman was seen, has now been exorcised.

Also in town a ghostly hand pushed around bottles and glasses in a pub bar ... while a head appeared through a wall ...

4

Two witches over a cauldron (1489)

MEANWHILE the Channel Islands continues to reveal dark secrets. Over the past 500 years there have been witchcraft trials, witchcraft arguments and people condemned as 'witches', mainly because they were old and their property was wanted by their next door neighbour.

Be that as it may, the modern form of 'witchcraft' is very different from what it has been in the past.

There are covens in Jersey. I thought there were only three but have been told that there are now four. But the people concerned don't necessarily label themselves as witches in the old traditional way. Simply put, they align themselves to an older tradition, one which predates Christianity.

So while 'Wicca' is a fairly modern term, in which adherents to this faith may pay homage to the sun and moon and often believe in the efficacy of ley lines, what follows is a definition of witchcraft in past and present times according to *Wikipedia*: 'Witchcraft (also called witchery or spell craft) is the use of alleged supernatural, magical faculties. This may take many forms, depending on cultural context.

'Beliefs in witchcraft have historically existed in most regions of the world. This was notably so in early modern Europe, where witchcraft came to be seen as part of a vast diabolical conspiracy of individuals in league with the Devil and undermining Christianity, eventually leading to large-scale witch-hunts, especially in Protestant Europe.

'The concept of witchcraft as harmful is normally treated as a cultural ideology providing a scapegoat for human misfortune.

'Since the mid-20th century witchcraft has become the designation of a branch of contemporary Paganism, most notably including Wiccan traditions, whose adherents claim to practise a revival of pre-Abramic spirituality.'

PROLOGUE

'Thou shalt not suffer a witch to live'

(Exodus, chapter 22, verse 18)

BETWEEN 1550 and 1661 at least 85 Channel Islanders were executed, condemned as witches. Some of them accepted their fate in belligerent style, admitting that they had cast spells on their neighbours or met at night at La Rocqueberg in Jersey or at Le Catioroc in Guernsey, where they said they entertained the Devil. One prisoner, for example, confessed to having killed a child, and another, Jean Morant, told how he had sacrificed a knuckle 'in tribute to his master'.

However, these were the minority, and most of these wrongdoers would have appeared in court at some stage of their lives for their sinful living, no matter what age they had been born into.

Meanwhile the majority of those arrested and executed may have been odd, immoral, old or superstitious but they were not evil. Instead they were victims of local law which had been created in the belief that the Devil and his disciples lived and breathed Channel Island air and would destroy the community unless they were dug out and destroyed.

Finding them was the problem, of course. By their very nature witches or Satanists were meant to be devious and cunning, able to tuck themselves away in the community while they went about their devilish work of harming cattle, destroying crops and casting spells on their neighbours so that they and their children would never know the meaning of good health.

They would also tell lies; and it would be a long, arduous process before a witch's resistance would be broken and the truth of his or her involvement with the Devil known.

This, then, was the attitude that the Island authorities adopted when a suspect was brought before them. When accused of *'la crime diabolique de sortilège'* your task was to prove yourself innocent, as best you could.

The jailer's task, on the other hand, was to prove that you were guilty and as you were 'put to the question' (i.e. tortured), the odds were always in the jailer's favour. He already knew that whatever you said (unless it was exactly what he wanted to hear) was a pack of lies and, if you didn't agree with his version of your wicked lifestyle, he had at his disposal certain pieces of equipment which would help to change your mind.

At the Beauregard Tower near St Peter Fort in Guernsey, for example, it was usual to interrogate a prisoner while he was tied to the strappado. This was a large, clumsy, hand-cranked machine which tore the victim's limbs from their sockets while the warder busied himself with turning the handle and jotting down the answers to his questions.

With a device such as this to speed up the legal process it is not surprising that admissions of guilt came remarkably quickly – once your muscles began to stretch, any desire you had to protect your innocence soon evaporated.

Some of the original confessions and court records still remain. They make fascinating reading and show that Islanders were genuinely concerned about the number of witches who appeared to be living in Guernsey.

They also show that at least one Guernsey greffier had a perverse sense of humour. For in the margins of the court records can be seen crudely drawn pictures of condemned prisoners dangling from the gibbets or surrounded by flames. Cartoons like these are graphic reminders that life was cheap in those days; which is one of the reasons why many Islanders decided to leave these shores and make a new life for themselves in America.

By 1692 the witch trials in Jersey and Guernsey were over – still remembered, perhaps, but mainly a thing of the past – and in New England many Channel Islanders, or their children, were doing extremely well for themselves.

Philip English (nee L'Anglois), for example, had his own fleet of ships which regularly sailed between Europe and the eastern seabord of America.

Business was good; and it would continue to be so unless something totally unexpected was to happen. It did, for the Devil arrived in Salem and, by the time he was laid to rest, Philip English was a shattered man, his wife was near to death and 19 New Englanders had been hanged as witch fever raged in the area.

So what follows is a history of Channel Island witchcraft, its origins and its travels. Against all the odds it has survived, although what we now call 'witchcraft' is not necessarily a faith that has links to the Devil. Nevertheless, so-called sorcery and divination have continued to cause all kinds of trouble, leading at times to the courts – but not to the stake.

Meanwhile modern-day 'Wicca' (a 20th century word) has been embraced by many people and, in 2013, Jersey's 'witches' plus the official witch of Salem have been happy to talk to the media to explain exactly what the word has meant to them. Not so those who preyed on the superstitions and fears of some Islanders who, by their very nature, lived in fear of the supernatural.

Both types of people we will meet again.

Part I
CHAPTER I

LIKE Jersey, Anglesey is an island whose history is rich and varied and whose inhabitants' ceremonies are open to many interpretations and although we do not know too much about them, we do know that Anglesea was conquered by the Romans on at least two occasions – in AD 61 and AD 71, first by Suetonius Paulinus and secondly by Agricola. Both invasions led to the prompt defeat of the people living there, although the first invasion finished, of necessity, fairly quickly, as the Roman army had to deal with a far more urgent enemy, Boudicca, the Queen of the Iceni, in the south.

At the time there were very few written accounts of the battles in Anglesey; the only one in any detail being that of the Roman writer Tacitus who, in the Tacitus Annals, writes: 'He (Suetonius Paulinus) prepared accordingly to attack the island of Mona (Anglesey), which had a considerable population of its own, while serving as a haven for refugees; and, in view of the shallow and variable channel, constructed a flotilla of boats with flat bottoms. By this method the infantry crossed; the cavalry, who followed, did so by fording or, in deeper water, by swimming at the side of their horses.

'On the shore stood the opposing army with its dense array of armed warriors, while between the ranks dashed women in black attire like the Furies, with hair dishevelled, waving brands. All round the Druids, lifting their hands to heaven and pouring forth dreadful imprecations, which scared our soldiers by the unfamiliar sight so that, as if their limbs were paralysed, they stood motionless and exposed to wounds.

'Then, urged by their general's appeal and mutual encouragements not to quail before a troop of frenzied women, the Romans bore the standards onwards, smote down all resistance, and wrapped the foe in the flame of his own brands. A force was set over the conquered, and the sacred groves, devoted to inhuman superstitions, were destroyed.

La Gran'mère du Chimquière (the Grandmother of the Cemetery), St Martin's churchyard, Guernsey

'The Druids indeed deemed it a duty to cover their altars with the blood of captives and to consult their deities through human entrails.'

Tacitus's description of the sacred groves and altars slaked in blood is similar to an account given by the Roman writer Lucan, writing about Julius Caesar's visit to a site near Marseilles in Southern Gaul: 'Interlacing boughs enclosed a space of darkness and cold shade, and banished the sunlight from above ... Gods were worshipped there with savage rites, the altars were heaped with hideous offerings, and every tree was sprinkled with human gore.'

'Fall from up there, Mary of Lihou!' was a cry allegedly made by witches practising their ritual at Le Catioroc in Guernsey

Piecing together other accounts, many of them written long after the Romans' influence, it seems clear that the native women were, indeed, seen as 'Furies' but, at the time Europe embraced many religions, our knowledge of which becomes hazier from one generation to the next. But the evidence that the Channel Islands have been lived in since Paleolithic times lies scattered around us, with all of the Islands (including Herm, which has a surprisingly large number of standing stones) containing granite and earthen reminders of long-dead civilisations.

The Islands contain impressive burial mounds plus reminders of the past including La Hougue Bie in Jersey and one or two carved images of gods and goddesses, their identies now long forgotten. These include a crudely carved stone menhir in Castel graveyard, Guernsey, which dates back to about 1,000 BC and La Gran'mère du Chimquière, which helps to form the gateway at St Martin's churchyard, also in Guernsey, and which dates back to about 600 BC.

Both figures, it is believed, represent the all-embracing pre-Christian goddess described by archaeologists as 'Earth Mother', and statues carved in her honour have been found in large numbers throughout Europe.

The idea of a protective and metaphorical 'Earth Mother' must have been an immense comfort in days gone by, giving meaning to a primitive world where so much of the universe would have seemed to have been created by magic rather than by a Christian God.

The Castel menhir and La Gran'mère might not be as refined as stone images fashioned in central or southern Europe, but they must have served their purpose just as well. In recent times La Gran'mère has been a favourite 'mother' to Guernsey girls and brides-to-be, who would wrap garlands of flowers around her ancient neck on their wedding day to ensure that their marriage would be both happy and fruitful.

In contrast to centuries long past, the idea of asking a carved piece of granite for good luck evokes no more than a passing smile or sigh, depending on your point of view. This wasn't always the case, though, for once upon a time Christianity would definitely have disapproved, partly because of its own insecurity and jealousies that anyone who was not a Christian must be viewed with suspicion and, therefore, whenever possible, be brought into line.

That Christianity did emerge from the pack with such intensity owes a great deal to Imperial Rome and to the outposts of the empire for a number of reasons, for the teachings of Christ and Christian ideology, including the concept of equality in the after-life, had an attraction to everyone, from the poorest serf to the richest baron. People gravitated towards anything that would offer a new hope ... especially as the late Roman Empire began to unravel.

With inherent failings within Roman Society and with a population drawn from all quarters of the known world, the single God concept (monotheism) had great appeal and, eventually, Christianity initiated a political change in philosophy in which God stood above both the Emperor and Rome itself, even though Christianity had similarities to other cults that had already gained widespread acceptance.

Mithraism, for example, derived from eastern Zoroastrianism in the belief that the son of the sun had also come to earth to rescue mankind from itself, was extremely popular in the Roman Legions and, as the army travelled throughout the empire, the acceptance of the monotheistic concept (and the story of the son of God coming to the world to save humanity) travelled with it.

The cult of Dionysus, one of the old gods of both Greeks and Romans, also had enough similarities to promote a slow conversion to Christianity.

Perhaps even the imperial cult (emperor worship) played its own part. Augustus himself was considered the son of a living god (Julius Caesar) and transcended his human existence to become a divine being after his death.

The Roman people had been exposed to enough religious ideas bearing similarities to Christ to make the possibility of the Son of God and saviour of humanity a believable and relatively easy concept to adopt.

However, while evidence of early Christian behaviour and practice is closely scrutinised and debated, it is known that Christians weren't always of like mind and beliefs. Several various sects with widely divergent schools of thought developed as the worship of Christ spread.

Though most of the pronounced deviations from the Catholic norm, including Donatism, Gnosticism, Arianism and Pelagianism, were fairly late developments, they are evidence of widely varying views and practices being part of Christianity throughout its rise.

Eventually, the Orthodox Church would gain supreme hold of the eastern empire, and Catholicism would reign in the west. The Catholic Church brought uniformity to the faith and established it as a public institution rather than small communities of individual followers.

And, as its powers increased, the Church was able to establish strict laws and religious doctrine and to attack and destroy 'heresy' whenever it saw fit. Never forget, though, that this was as much a political policy as one based in religion.

The early Christians, having been persecuted themselves in centuries gone by, recognised that to survive and prosper they needed

14

to condemn all other religious faiths, no matter how deeply their roots lay.

Over a period of time Catholicism virtually destroyed all other sects and Paganism along with it.

HOWEVER, how do you destroy faiths and religions far older and more influential than your own?

Well, as has been mentioned earlier, early Christians, facing scorn at best and persecution at worst and in order to celebrate the 'holidays' (holy days) of their religion, adopted existing holidays and festivals to help lend new meaning to ritual occasions that had endured for many centuries before.

Christmas, for example, was originally part of the great festival of the Winter Solstice, or the Saturnalia. But by adopting this grand event as the celebration of Christ's birth, over a period of time the old ways became, if not forgotten, subservient to the new.

The Church, too, manipulated customs and traditions of the pagan empire to make their faith more adaptable. The one-time universally popular deity Cernnuous (the 'horned one'), for example, was renamed and then reviled as the Devil; All Saints Day (often called All Hallows) was switched from 3 May to 1 November in the eighth century to make it coincide with and to Christianise Samain, an important date in the Celtic calendar. On 31 October (Hallowe'en), for a fleeting period, the 'otherworld' of spirits and gods was thought to become visible to mankind.

Beliefs as powerful as these were not easy to destroy, but Christianity was determined to crush all other opposition, which is one of the reasons why the office of the Pope became both spiritually and temporally so important. Eventually, the Pope's power was so extraordinary that kings and emperors had to bow down before him. This, from a religion that at one time saw powerless Christians being thrown to the lions!

So Christianity grew and grew in its power and influence, especially when Charlemagne, King of the Franks from 768 AD and of Italy from 774, subdued the Saxons and Bavarians, pushed his frontier into Spain and then continued his father's policy towards the Papacy, becoming its protector and removing and mounting a war against the European Muslims. He made his enemies but unlike other powerful forces yet to come, he tolerated heretics as long as they did not threaten Christian beliefs and territories.

As other Christian scholars beforehand, he recognised that one of the best ways to convert his people was to build churches on what had once been 'pagan' grounds and to impose Christian dates on those of older religions, to lesser or greater effect and for many of the centuries to follow. This became a Christian trait; to burn out the old ways and old ceremonies and to build churches on hallowed ground which, previously, had been groves sacred to religions going back many hundreds of years before Christ.

Does this have any relevance to Jersey? Perhaps, because it is believed that the Anglican Church of St Mary was built on a sacred grove where, once upon a time, Islanders would meet and pray ... to other gods.

So what has any of this to do with the witch hunts which spread like wildfire through Europe between the 15th and 18th centuries during which time those accused of witchcraft were portrayed as being worshippers of the Devil, who engaged in sorcery and attended witches' sabbats before being tried, jailed and afterwards 'tested'? As we will see, Pope Innocent VIII in the latter part of the 15th century had a great deal to do with this. And a brief history of the Channel Islands shows that there is an air of inevitability that witch trial mania would eventually arrive in such a close community off Britain's most southerly shores.

THE total number of Islanders or strangers to the Islands who were executed before the 15th century is a matter of dispute – not least because Devil worship and witches at one time, and even now, were not necessarily thought to have the same origins. And, in a more forgiving era of the 20th and 21st centuries, many 'witches' will insist they are as Christian as any other parishioner who goes to church. You can even 'talk' to them on the internet. In October 2007, in an interview for the BBC, Rhianna Galvin, admitted that she was a practising Wicca ('Wicca' is a 20th century term. Adherents use dolmens for rituals based on the setting sun and rising moon) but said that with 'witchcraft there's no control – there's no guilt, there's no fear factor'. She is also a busy mum, medium and clairvoyant; she lives by the seasons; is very conscious of the planet that we live on and how we live, and 'very conscious of how I am with other people because we believe in the three-fold law: that whatever we send out comes back to us three times'.

Also, her main role in life, outside her immediate family, is to help other people.

This 'three-fold law' – that whatever you give out (usually in the form of a wish or, occasionally, in the form of a curse) will come back to do triple harm or triple good to the 'witch' who made that wish is also a faith that the official witch of Salem, Laurie Cabot, adheres to while, as Rhianna blithely pointed out, there is nothing devilish in 'Wicca' for 'you can go into any bookshop these days and buy white witch good spells and things like that ...'

You can, too. But to even think of doing so 500 years ago would lead you into all kinds of trouble. Before then? Well ... look at the history of the Islands and judge for yourself.

BETWEEN 8000 and 6500 BC the Channel Islands were separated from mainland Europe. Round about the same time Neolithic people moved here and Neolithic tombs and standing stones, megaliths and dolmens were built, many centuries before Christ.

Other invaders were to either pillage or stay here, bringing their gods with them. They included the Beaker People, the Vikings, the Gauls, the Celts and, by 525AD, Christian Bretons.

In 555AD St Helier, one of several Christian missionaries to the Channel Islands, was killed by marauding pirates; in 568AD St Magloire's monastery was founded in Sark; from 800 to 911AD the Vikings would often invade. Then from 931 to 1204AD the Channel Islands were ruled from Rouen as part of Normandy.

In 1204 King John lost his Norman territories but, miraculously, kept the Channel Islands; in the 14th century the Black Death struck; between 1461 and 1468 the French occupied the Channel Islands; in 1483 a Papal Bull decreed that they would be neutral during time of war before; a year later, Pope Innocent VIII issued the Papal Bull, Summis Desiderantes Affectibus, which stressed that witchcraft was a Christian heresy and the greatest of all sins

'Many a farmer walking back to his cottage would go a mile further rather than approach the rock' (La Rocqueberg in Jersey, which is said to have been 'marked by the Devil')

because it led to the renunciation of God and worship of His greatest enemy.

Times had changed and the tolerance shown by Charlemagne was now long forgotten. And, by this time, it was assumed that just as black is the opposite of white so if there was a God there must be a Devil – although the Channel Islands were rarely at the forefront of the European and British witch and heresy trials.

As they have always done, these islands lagged a little way behind, although certain influential Islanders and ministers were to make up for their tardiness and to write laws, too, which echoed those of the continent and of Britain.

So it was that the major period for witchcraft trials was between 1552 and 1736, with one of the pricipal Jersey anti-witchcraft laws being extended and elaborated in December 1591 when the Royal Court of Jersey issued a proclamation that any Islander 'consulting a witch for any reason, medical or otherwise, was as bad as being a witch yourself; whereas many have in days gone by committed the heinous sin of seeking aid in times of trouble from warlocks

Faldouet in Jersey which has been exorcised on more than one occasion and which is said to be part of a ley line which was 'tapped into' by pre-Christian Islanders

and witches, a thing contrary to the order of God and his express command, and a grievous insult to the Christian faith ... and whose duty it is to administer justice ... and whereas ignorance is no excuse for sin and no one can tell what depravity and danger may ensure from such practices in order that henceforth all may turn from these wicked and devilish cures ... the use of which merits by God's law the same penalty as is inflicted on warlocks and witches themselves, and that God's wrath may be averted which now threatens the officers of justice because of the impunity with which these crimes are committed [so that] all who dwell in this Island are strictly forbidden to receive aid or advice in trouble from witches or warlocks or anyone suspected of witchcraft and of paying a month's imprisonment in the castle [Mont Orgueil] on dried bread and water with the reservation that they must declare in court their excuse for such effrontery and accordingly be dealt with reasonably as God's law directs.'

In other words, the Royal Court taught that witchcraft and Satanism were one and the same thing and that if you were tempted to go to a 'witch' (a word many Islanders may well have substituted as 'a wise woman'), you were as guilty of Devil worship as they were. Such a crime could only have been punishable if European and English courts were coming to the same conclusion too; although there was at least one woman, Perrine Alixandre, the wife of Estienne Bertault, who beat the court system, according to the Cour de Cattel ledgers at the Jersey Archive, by living a rather miserable life, but living it according to the letter of the law.

For although she was not immediately put on trial she was arrested as a witch and ordered to be sent to the castle for a month on bread and water before the court believed, it must be assumed, that she would then plead guilty.

She didn't. Instead, as it was her right to do, she rejected one of the jurors set to try her case, probably on spurious grounds but on grounds that the magistrate couldn't ignore.

After all, it was a right the courts had given her, once a trial had been set. Another month followed and again she complained about one of her intended jurors and was consequently returned to the castle … and so it went on for a year as the so-called 'witch' lived on a frugal diet of bread and water, constantly rejecting one juror after another before eventually the Court tired of this game. And so it was that she was released with a warning.

That wouldn't happen today of course …'witchcraft' has been superseded by threats with violence, attempted blackmail and divination. However, just as Tacitus marveled at the 'Furies' in Anglesey in AD61, almost 2,000 years later, Islanders and mainlanders alike aren't so different in some of the beliefs they hold. It might not seem in any way diabolic or threatening, but how many people read their horoscopes, or salute a magpie if they see one? This may have little to do with witchcraft, but it has a great deal to do with our own superstitious nature ... and, burn as many Islanders as you like, you cannot stop them from believing, perhaps, that they are cursed or ill-fated ... as we will soon discover.

Chapter 2

IN the Channel Islands paganism had begun its slow decline from about the fifth century AD, when Celtic tribesmen left southern Britain and crossed to a large devastated area in western France known as Armorica. These were the Breton folk, and they and the Christian missionaries who accompanied them were to have a profound effect on the area for Brittany still bears their name and Bretons, even today, are very different from their close French neighbours.

Ironically, when the Bretons were settling in this part of the world they were rejoining other Celts, not running away from them, for some of their neighbours both in mainland France and the Channel Islands were descended from the Coriosolites, a Celtic tribe which had settled on the western seaboard of Europe 300 years and more before Christ was born.

So Celts were reunited with Celts, and that Celtic culture must have been very strong for several centuries as Christianity dug its roots in the Islands, aided by missionaries such as St Magloire, St Sampson, St Tugual and the fanatical Christian recluse, St Helier. St Brelade (known in the sixth century as Branwalader or 'Raven's Lord') also visited the Islands, where he is supposed to have observed the antics of pagan Guernseymen with interest, commenting that they were the most devoted adherents to the 'Old Religion' that he had ever seen.

At the time neither he, nor his fellow Christian travellers, would have been able to undermine the old beliefs, either by force or argument, and it must be remembered that for many centuries after the death of Christ the Christian faith accommodated pagan practices in a way that 16th and 17th century Christians would have deplored.

It was not until the seventh century AD, for example, that the Archbishop of Canterbury felt secure enough to prohibit sacrifice to devils, eating and drinking in heathen temples, and wearing stag or bull skins at honorary kalends (festivals). For this last offence he was prepared to impose a sentence of three years' penance be-

The Norsemen brought their own sorcerers to the Islands, including Frigg, who could 'turn the evil eye' on an enemy

cause it was 'Devilish behaviour'. He also imposed a special penance for charming, making love philtres, poisoning or 'making vows at a clump of trees, at a spring, at certain rocks or at a spot where boundaries meet'.

In out-of-the-way places such as the Channel Islands such pagan practices would have continued, virtually unchecked for many years. Christianity may have rooted itself here but it was a Christianity shaped to the needs and superstitions of a Celtic race and, as Tacitus explained, the Celt may have had an air of nobility about

Then there was Freyja, who could turn herself into human form and allegedly slept with *all* of the northern dwarves

him but he was also moody, bone-idle, save when hunting or at war and plunder, and living a tribal way of life that was totally incompatible with ordered civilisation. Celts, he decided, dismissing them out of hand, might have been good farmers but they were also extremely hairy and incredibly superstitious.

This Celtic culture was to survive well into the ninth century when another visitor came, fought and stayed – the North or Norse man. Initially travelling south from cold Scandinavian countries by longboat, he was different in looks and nature to the existing Channel Islander. Northmen were fatalistic, dour, pragmatic, with a passion for litigation and with gods who were as cold and insensitive as the bleak northern nights.

Like Celtic tribesmen, they were superstitious and suspicious of their neighbours but, unlike them, they were uninterested in farming, and their attitude to foreigners, to women, to life, death and to each other was bleak in the extreme.

A flavour of their attitude to the way of the world, and to an interesting burial custom, can be found in John Bowle's 'A History of Europe' (London, 1979). Bowle writes: 'On the Volga in the early tenth century, slave girls would voluntary die with their masters, along with horses and cattle. To the thumping of staves on shields the girls, bemused with drink, would be ritually violated by successive warriors, muttering thickly if unconvincingly "tell your master I have done this out of love for him".

'The unfortunate girl would then be strangled, and finished off by an old woman known as the Angel of Death, who knifed her between the ribs. More simply, they would bury a dead man's favourite wife alive and unprotesting beside him.'

With visitors like these to contend with, no wonder the Islanders dreaded the Vikings' summer excursions but, by the tenth century, the Northman was prepared to make a more permanent home in western France and he was doing so by migrating in numbers south through mainland Europe.

The leader of the Northmen who ruthlessly cut their way towards western France was named Rollo. By 911AD he forced Charles the Simple of France to cede a large slice of land to him to the southwest of Paris and in 933AD his son, William Longsword, added to this territory so that from then until 1204 'the land of the Bretons by the sea coast' (including the Channel Islands) was part of the Duchy of Normandy: the Normans had arrived.

It must have been a heady mixture, this combination of Celtic and Norman civilisation, and although they both shared a common religion – Christianity – for the early Norman warrior (it would be wrong to call him 'settler' because it was a long time before the Normans settled into a peaceful, rustic way of life) conversions to the Christian faith were often tentative and political.

An excellent example of this easy-come, easy-go attitude to the church can be found in Lewis Thorne's 'Einhard and Notker the Stammerer: Two Lives of Charlemagne' (Harmondsworth, 1969) when an old Scandinavian warrior complains at the Court of King Louis the Pious that the clothes he has been given to go with his conversion are of terrible quality.

He continues: 'This old sack makes me feel more like a pig farmer than a soldier. If it weren't for the fact that you've pinched my own clothes and not given me any new ones, so that I should feel a right fool if I walked out of here naked, you could keep your Christ and your suit of hand-me-downs, too!'

Memories of northern gods who had little to do with Christianity would have stayed with the Normans as they arrived in the Islands. There was Odin, the sky father, who could send his spirit across the skies and make it appear as a bird or small animal hundreds of miles away; the Valkyries, 'choosers of the slain', who, like the Druid priests in Anglesey, predicted the fate of men by studying bloody entrails; and Freyja, a goddess who was translated into the Christian faith as the archetypal witch and who symbolised much of the folklore associated with northern sorcery.

As well as being highly promiscuous (she was given a rare jewel as reward for sleeping with all of the northern dwarves), she was thought to be a shamanka who, in human form, could house a woman's soul and a spirit from the other side in one body – thereby being a medium between our world and the unknown, but being at peace in neither.

Shamans (male) and shamankas (female) were an accepted part of northern life for many centuries before and after Christianity became rooted in Europe, and if such men and women didn't arrive in the Channel Islands with the Vikings and the Normans, knowledge of them certainly did.

Like Celtic priests they were well-respected members of their community, believed to have the gift of prophecy, to have miraculous healing powers, and to be able to turn the 'evil eye' against anyone who stood in their path.

Men and women like Freyja and her shaman following have always existed, of course, and they can still be found in various primitive societies throughout the world, particularly in the southern hemisphere. But it could be argued that what came to be called 'witchcraft' owes a great deal to our Celtic and Norman ancestry. Both races were extremely superstitious and flourished in a community cut off from the rest of Europe in which their superstitions were unlikely to be challenged over the years.

And why should they have been? Who could deny them? As long as the Bishop of Coutances received his tithes he was satisfied before, in 1204, his influence was severely curtailed when Normandy became part of France and, two years later, the Channel Islands became part of England.

Despite French bishops retaining religious control of the Islands, once they were confirmed as King John's property, no French bishop would enjoy crossing the sea to deal with erring parishioners, especially when the French and English were at war (which happened all too often).

Any intervention, either spiritual or physical, would have been seen as an insult to the English Crown (it may have been the right thing to do from an ecumenical point of view but, in practice, it was foolhardiness in the extreme).

So, when religious controversy raged in the rest of Europe, life in the Channel Islands carried on pretty much as it had always done. Outside influences weren't appreciated and it must have been easier, and more satisfying, to consult a local Christian minister or, if that failed, to go to the local wise woman if spiritual advice was needed.

Such reliance on both the old ways and the new caused no heartache to an Island race, which was used to compromise and which saw no conflict in a combination of Christianity and native superstition.

This combination would have appalled any new visitor to the Channel Islands at the beginning of the 16th century, in particular French Protestants, often called Huguenots. Devoted to a Christianity which detested superstition and unnecessary ritual, they would have been incensed by an apparent lack of respect for Christ and a reliance instead on 'Devilish practices'.

Superstition and sorcery would have to go – which is one of the

The Devil: who appeared variously as a goat, as a black man, or as 'a man in animal form'

reasons why there were so many witch trials in the 16th and 17th centuries. But you cannot destroy superstition so easily, so, on the reasonable assumption that if prayer of one sort doesn't guarantee success, why not try another. Let us end this chapter with a true account of the Reverend Thomas Brock's first encounter with a side of his congregation he had never seen before.

In Guernsey, some time in 1804, the new incumbent of the rectory at St Pierre-du-Bois, the Rev Brock, was returning from St Peter Port late one night when he was amazed to see a number of people gathered near the church porch.

With some trepidation he tied his horse to the gate and stepped over the stile into the churchyard. As he neared the church he had to shake his head, to make sure he wasn't dreaming, for the most extraordinary ceremony he had ever seen was taking place. Several of his parishioners were moving around the building in some sort of organised procession, touching every angle as they passed.

Not unnaturally, the Reverend Brock asked what they were doing but no-one would answer his questions. Perfect silence was maintained until the group came to the church porch where they all knelt down and recited the Lord's Prayer. This was repeated several times before the group drifted away, leaving the rector none the wiser and less than happy with the antics of his congregation.

Early next morning he called in on one or two of those who had taken part in the previous night's ritual.

He was told that the ceremony was designed to remove a spell which had been placed on the daughter of one of Rev Brock's congregation – a single word out of place and the counter-charm would have been broken ...

Ritual such as this was all part of an Islander's way of life; it helped to form his character and, left alone, didn't cause too much harm in the neighbourhood.

However, if any Islander had been caught practising such ritual 250 years earlier, he would have faced a sterner inquisitor than the mild-mannered Thomas Brock. Instead, he would have been hauled away to Beauregard Tower and questioned in such a way that he would confess to anything. Torture, you see, was a prerequisite when cross-examining one of the Devil's children.

Chapter 3

SO let us move on now to a different era ... for between the Norman Conquest and the Reformation no more than half a dozen supposed witches were executed, most of them accused of being involved in plots against the monarch or his friends.

Other so-called witches were never brought to trial because, in pre-Reformation society, there were good witches as well as bad so, if your child was ill, you would almost certainly take him or her to the 'wise woman' in your community – many of whom had more knowledge about herbal cures than anyone else in the village.

All of this was to change, largely because of the Reformation, although the Catholic Church in Europe also became preoccupied with the apparent heresy of 'witchcraft', which was supposedly guided and controlled by the Devil.

For this the blame or, depending on your point of view, approval, lies initially with Pope Innocent VIII.

Zealous but superstitious and dogged by a political battle which was to trouble him throughout his lifetime, he also had to look after a flock which, on his succession in 1484, was facing huge difficulties of its own.

For what we now call the Little Ice Age, the grip of freezing weather, the failure of crops and a rise in crime in the 1480s, led to mass starvation ... leading, in turn, to Catholics wanting an explanation for such a downturn in their fortunes.

The explanation was, the Pope decided, a combination of witchcraft and Satanism and, unlike Catholic priests from the past, he generously and unequivocably linked the two.

It was he, for example, who confirmed Tomas de Torquemada as the Grand Inquisitor of Spain, so that, initially, the Spanish Inquisition had Rome's blessing.

And it was Pope Innocent VIII whose 1484 Papal Bull, Summis Desiderantes Affectibus (Desiring with Supreme Ardour), stressed that witchcraft was a Christian heresy, the greatest of all sins, because it led to the renunciation of God and worship of His greatest enemy.

**A witch and her familiar from De Laniis et Phitonicis
Mulieribus (1489)**

Remembering how far Papal influence extended in those days,
across the whole of Europe (and, until Henry VIII broke from the
Catholic faith with the Act of Supremacy in 1534, in England too),
Germany and Spain were to bear the brunt of a systematic pursuit
of witches, white or black, some of whom could trace their legacy
to a faith established many centuries before Christ was born.

The Pope's decree, on its own, might have been less than effec-
tive if Pope Innocent VIII hadn't listened to two Germanic Dominican Inquisitors, Heinrich Kramer and James Sprenger, who
published the 'Malleus Maleficarum' (the 'Hammer of the
Witches') in 1486 and who included 'Summis Desiderantes Affectibus' in their foreword.

Their work makes for potent reading: 'Many persons of both sexes, unmindful of their own salvation and straying from the Catholic faith, have abandoned themselves to devils, incubi and succubi, and by their incantations, spells, conjurations, and other accursed charms and crafts, enormities and horrid offences, have slain infants yet in the mother's womb, as also the offspring of cattle, have blasted the produce of the earth, the grapes of the vine, the fruits of the trees, nay, men and women, beasts of burthen, herd-beasts, as well as animals of other kinds, vineyards, orchards, meadows, pasture-land, corn, wheat, and all other cereals … these torment men and women, beasts of burthen, herd-beasts, as well as animals of other kinds, with terrible and piteous pains and sore diseases … they hinder men from performing the sexual act and women from conceiving, whence husbands cannot know their wives nor wives receive their husbands … and at the instigation of the Enemy of Mankind they do not shrink from committing and perpetrating the foulest abominations and filthiest excesses …'

Initially the publication had no real general effect. Kramer, for example, was thrown out of the Tyrol by the local bishop, who described the author as a 'senile old man', but 30 years beforehand Johannes Gutenberg had invented a device which was to give the book more power than its authors could ever have contemplated – the printing press.

Between 1487 and 1520, 20 editions of the 'Malleus' were published and English translations are being published even today.

So, although the book was eventually denounced by the Church and by the Inquisition, its effect on European society was to take a heavy toll.

With the underlying belief that all 'witches' were unquestionably in league with the Devil, the 'Malleus' explained how to detect them while also giving, in graphic detail, a few handy hints about how to recognise them. For example, if women did not cry during their trial, jurors were advised that the Devil was almost certainly inside them.

Women were most suited to witchcraft … but why not men? Well, because the authors advised that women were more susceptible to temptation than their husbands, which is partly why even the title of the book is in a feminine tense. For 'Maleficarum' is a 'female' word. The male equivalent is 'Maleficorum'.

After its publication and for the next 200 years the 'old days' of Charlemagne who, in the 8th and 9th centuries, had specifically outlawed the old practice of witch burning 'in the manner of the pagans', were both forgotten and ignored.

Meanwhile, the Catholic Church had soon to contend with yet another enemy – the Reformation – led, in part, by Martin Luther (1483-1546) whose Protestantism undoubtedly did a huge amount of good (for example, Luther was adamant that no-one could buy their way out of Hell), but who also preached that the world of visible reality and of the flesh belonged to the Devil.

So, for many English Protestants, Satan became a greater physical reality than ever before – 'the Prince and God of this world' John Knox called him – while preachers of all Christian denominations would tell their congregation of foul and diabolic practices occurring within the heart of their community. And as Hugh Latimer assured his audience that the Devil and his company of evil spirits were invisible in the air around them ('I am not able to tell how many thousand there are among us'), James I vilified Satan as 'God's hangman'.

His philosophy, King James believed, had already stood the test of time, though it was partly based on the Elizabethan Communion service, a communion during which the priest told sinners not to come to the table 'lest after taking of that holy sacrament the Devil enter into you'.

And so it was that during this period there were many examples of preachers identifying members of their congregation who were supposedly beset by devils, including Thomas Wilkinson, minister of Helminham, Norfolk, who told a child of his congregation that the 'Devil was upon his shoulders' – which in turn led to the boy rushing out of the church, screaming in terror. Catholicism and the Puritan faith came together to preach against witchcraft and encouraged sermons to be preached against the Devil, the two faiths now firmly entrenched in the belief that witches and Satanism were part and parcel of the same thing. Even King James wrote a treatise against witchcraft on succeeding to the throne.

CHAPTER 4

WITHIN a lifetime of James's condemnation of witchcraft three Acts of Parliament were published which made sorcery a statutory offence.

The first was in 1542, repealed in 1547, which made it a capital offence to conjure spirits or to practise witchcraft. The second law was in 1563 (repealed in 1604) which emphasised the maleficent nature of a witch's activities for invoking evil spirits for any purpose whatsoever. (Prior to that, if no one had died through sorcery, a 'witch' may well have walked free or been given a much lighter sentence).

Then, in 1604, a new law made it illegal to have any communication with evil spirits or animal familiars, and harming, rather than killing a neighbour, became punishable by death.

According to that 1604 law, a second offence for such trivial matters as lost goods, unlawful love, destroying cattle or goods, taking up a dead body in whole or part for 'magical' purposes (which helped delay any advances in medical science for over a century), and to 'consult, covenant with, entertain, employ, feed, or reward any evil and wicked spirit to or for any intent or purpose' could also lead to execution.

Such a heinous law was to remain on the statute books until 1736, although its effectiveness often depended not so much on the 'crime' but in the area in which you lived and by whom you had been accused.

For example, 492 indictments for maleficent witchcraft were recorded at the Essex Assizes in the 1640s, many of them instigated by the self-proclaimed 'witchfinder-general', Matthew Hopkins, who between 1645 and 1647 helped secure the arrest and conviction of over 200 people.

Hopkins is a curious example of a man who, while undoubtedly believing in Satanism and witchcraft, also made an exceptional living from his gruesome 'day job', as he charged £23 (the equivalent of £6,700 in 2013) for services at Stowmarket. And Ipswich had to levy a special local tax before they could pay for his services.

Frontispiece of Matthew Hopkins's 'The Discovery of Witches' (1647), showing witches with their familiar spirits

The son of a Puritan clergyman, Hopkins was to make his home in Essex and first came to public notice after 1634 when Charles I ordered his physician, William Harvey, to examine four women in Lancashire, each one of whom had been accused of making a pact with the Devil. For so many years before this trial, witches were usually treated similarly to those of other criminals; but once the law courts, advised by the clergy, determined that witches owed their powers to Satan, rather than to God, it was decreed that witchcraft was a *crimen excepta* (a crime so horrid that all normal legal procedures went to the wall), which in turn allowed that witchcraft confessions could be gained by torture.

After all, if the Devil was within the women on trial, it would take a great deal of persuasion to persuade him to leave.

So it was that by 1645 Hopkins had declared himself Parliament's 'official' witch-finder (without Parliament's permission). But few questioned this because, by now, England was engulfed by the Civil War (Charles I would be executed in January 1649). In retrospect, we can say that Hopkins was lucky, for, at the time of his Inquisition, normal society was largely in free-fall.

With Civil War came fear and a society turning in upon itself, which is perhaps why in March 1645 23 women accused of witch-craft and tried at Chelmsford were found guilty by a court presided over by the Earl of Warwick. Four died in prison before the other 19 were convicted and hanged.

Fellow 'witch-finder' John Stearne and his friend Hopkins were instrumental in the 'examination' of these so-called witches and, soon afterwards Hopkins wrote and had published in 1647 'The Discovery of Witches'.

It was and is a vile book, detailing how the accused should be subjected to examination. Although torture was illegal in England, Hopkins ignored this completely, blithely suggesting that sleep deprivation was one way to extract a confession. Other ways included the swimming test, by which women would be bound to a chair and thrown into the water ... if they drowned they were innocent, if they floated they were guilty ... plus the novel idea that if you cut the arm of the accused with a blunt knife and she did not bleed, she, too, was guilty of being a witch.

The book Hopkins wrote was, and is, horrendous, with its inclusion of a detailed description of how to find 'the Devil's mark'. Witches, Hopkins decreed, would almost certainly possess a piece of flesh which was dead to all feeling and would not bleed; or perhaps a witch would have a mole or a birthmark. Both signs of a witch's compact with Satan.

And if the suspected witch had no such visible marks, those marks could well be invisible and could invariably be discovered by pricking with special needles used to look for the Devil's mark upon the body, normally after the suspect had been shaved of all bodily hair.

While some enlightened churchmen and scholars poured scorn on Hopkins's thesis, others pronounced it as fact and incorporated his ideas into their law books, some of which eventually found their way to the New England colonies in America.

As described in the journal of Massachusetts Governor John Winthrop (who, in 1605 had married an Essex girl), evidence assembled against Margaret Jones was gathered by the use of Hopkins's techniques of 'searching' and 'watching' during a witch-hunt that was to last between 1648 and 1663 and which saw 80 people accused, of whom 15 women and two men were executed. A further witch-hunt between 1692 and 1693 in Salem would result in 150 imprisonments and 19 executions.

As for Hopkins? In 1647, the same year that his book was published, he was to die of tuberculosis. He hadn't even turned 30. But, in death as in life, he was a controversial figure who provoked popular comment about whether he was truly a man of God or, perhaps, a Satanist who took great delight in condemning God's children and then having the satisfaction of seeing them die.

This is not to say that the government of the day, fragmented as it was, plus local clergymen, agreed with his beliefs and writings. It was mentioned in Parliament that he had unlawfully claimed to be their representative, while the Reverend John Stearn wrote his 'Select Cases of Conscience Touching Witches and Witchcrafts' in 1646, a book which refuted Hopkins's theories after one of his congregation had been accused of Satanism.

For this accusation against a parishioner he believed was truly Christian, Stearn was incensed, even though it wasn't that he disbelieved in witchcraft. Instead he questioned Hopkins's methods of examination while also complaining bitterly about his charges.

Stearn suggested alternatives, which is why his book, too, was used during the Salem witch trials held between February 1692 and May 1693.

It was believed that a 'witch' had to be burnt and then the ashes thrown to the 'four points of the compass'

CHAPTER 5

IN the previous chapter we have seen how, by the 15th century, the Church had lumped witchcraft and the Devil together, as if they were part and parcel of the very same thing. They weren't.

However, the Papal Bull of 1484 followed by the English laws approved by government in 1542, 1563 and 1604, were all based on the premise that the Devil lived and flourished throughout the known world and they gave the Church and its leaders the right to conduct any 'examination' needed, including the use of torture, to weed out Satanists in their church congregation or in their community at large.

All of this was a far cry from earlier years when 'witchcraft' was generally tolerated (unless it led to someone's death) before Satanism became another matter entirely. For example, in 1303 the philosopher Robert of Brunne might have issued warnings against offering sacrifices to the Devil but those who did so were not necessarily considered as witches. They were Satanists, and there is a huge difference between the two words and their meanings.

Not that this made any difference to the witch-finders of any town, county or country and if the Church told you there were evil folk among you, even your next door neighbour might be reported to them or to the civil authorities. For if, for example, a child was still-born or if the crops failed, it was easier to blame your neighbour or to blame the weird woman you had consulted … the 'weird woman' being someone who had some idea about the potency of herbs while also believing in magic.

Such women were often accepted in a community while that community thrived but were vilified when there was a plague or drought. For a long time such women were tolerated, though perhaps treated with suspicion, and it wasn't until the 15th century onwards that the Church suggested such people were in league with the Devil.

So, following the Pope's 1484 Papal Bull, 'Summis Desiderantes Affectibus', Catholics and then Protestants were assured that witchcraft and Satanism were endemic in most European countries.

However, in Britain the witchcraft trials of the 16th and 17th centuries might never have led to so many people's deaths or imprisonments if a) there weren't laws and the Church to guide their persecution b) if there weren't the likes of Matthew Hopkins, the Earl of Warwick and the Catholic church to consider judgement and c) communities were not encouraged to turn in upon themselves when, only a few generations before, those self-same communities looked after each other – parishioners helping, rather than condemning, less fortunate people than themselves who lived in the town or village.

For as Keith Thomas writes in 'Religion and the Decline of Magic' (Penguin): 'Whereas once upon a time villagers would happily consult a "wise woman" in their community; someone who could help cure their children, often because they had a far greater understanding of the healing powers of certain plants than anyone else in the village ...

'Now it was rumoured that their curing powers had been given to them by the Devil. Similarly, there were certain villagers who would cast spells or practise magic, the irony being that while the magic was believed to emanate from God by those who indulged in such practices ... the suspicion was that any cures that worked did so because the "weird woman" was in league with the Devil while, if the cures didn't work and a child died, this, too, was Satan's work.'

Basing law on superstition and effectively asking the questions 'Can your next door neighbour really be trusted? And why is it, for example, that your crops haven't thrived this year and that your youngest child is dead?' turned communities in upon themselves and it only needed a zealous clergyman or town or village elder to accept that one neighbour might well be right in thinking that another neighbour was using the Devil's powers to destroy them.

For by now they had laws to accuse, to examine, and to condemn.

In 'Religion and the Decline of Magic' Thomas gives copious examples of how such practices might work. In a chapter headed 'Witchcraft and its Social Environment' he writes: '(their) depositions show that the accuser established the witch's identity in one of a few standard ways.

'Usually the victim would recall a threat uttered by someone with whom he had recently quarreled. He might even have nocturnal visions of "the witch" or cry out in his fits against his supposed persecutor. In 1653 the six-year-old son of Edward Hodge, labourer, of Benenden, Kent, began to have strange attacks in the night, calling out "Father, father, here comes a black hairy thing which will tease and kill me". When he added: "Bess Wood ... she will kill me," his parents knew that he had been bewitched by Elizabeth Wood, who already had a reputation for witchcraft and who had recently quarreled with the son's mother.

'Possessed persons were often called upon to name the person who had afflicted them and, after a little coaxing, (they) could usually be prevailed upon to do so. Thus in 1626 Edward Dynham fell into a trance, speaking in three different voices, in one of which, after some encouragement, he revealed the identity of the witches who were tormenting him, and, he said, had already destroyed one victim. The two accused persons, Edward Bull and Joan Creedie, were duly indicted at Taunton Assizes. Any doubt about their guilt was removed when a gentlewoman, seized with a mysterious shaking in her side, cried out "Bull, bull!" (while) more rarely the sight of a toad or some apparent animal familiar in the suspect's house might trigger off an accusation; or the confession of one witch might incriminate another.'

The Devil was everywhere ... including the Channel Islands ... although many Channel Island trials ignored trivia, which was not so in Lancashire in 1582 when Alice Baxter rushed to her employer to complain that the Devil had revealed himself to her when a cow she was milking had kicked away her pail.

Three years later the widow Margaret Harkett was executed at Tyburn after picking a basketful of peas in a neighbour's field without asking for permission.

Asked to return them, she 'flung them down in anger since when no peas would grow in the field'. Later, she was struck by a bailiff who had caught her taking wood from his master's ground. Allegedly, the bailiff then went mad. 'Another parishioner, underpaid her for a pair of shoes; later he died,' the court was told: 'After which her neighbours were unable to make butter and cheese ...'

Obviously she was a witch and so it was that the 60-year-old Mrs Harkett duly died at the gallows.

There would be similar, occasional outbursts of witchcraft fury in Guernsey and Jersey. (Why, for example, would cattle in a field in St Ouen not thrive and would die? Because it was later discovered, the earth contained an enormous amount of salt.) What was more than peculiar was the number of self-proclaimed witches, including Collas Becquet in the Channel Island and Giles Fenderlyn in the UK. The latter, when examined by Hopkins, claimed in 1652 to be entertaining his familiar in jail, even though no other observer could see it.

Then there was the butcher, Meggs, who voluntarily travelled from 12 miles away in Essex to be searched by Hopkins before he, too, was duly executed as a witch, all of which prompted the writer and philosopher Thomas Hobbes to shake his head in disbelief and say: 'Though I cannot believe in witches, yet I cannot believe there are none, by reason that they themselves confess it.'

So why confess? Well, Keith Thomas points out that in times of great hardships, parishioners admitted their guilt because their lives were so meaningless they had little to lose by appealing to the Devil when all else had failed to make their lives less miserable. Also, it was possible to frighten a neighbour into giving them what they asked for if they let it be known that if they didn't do so, they would be punished by their Master ... a concept we will return to shortly.

However, it is also important to remember that not every town or county saw devils everywhere around them or took their neighbours to court for turning against God while some magistrates, too, scoffed at the 'witch' laws; one of them, for example, telling the court that 'as there is no law against flying', the 'witch' before him would be allowed to go free.

Such a tongue-in-cheek approach might not have met with the courts' approval but, by the early 18th century there were enough scholars and free thinkers to pour scorn on 'witchcraft' in any number of ways.

Reginald Scot, for example, quoted the Cleves physician Johan Weyer's 'De Pre-assigning Daemonum' (1563) to urge that many supposed witches were innocent 'melancholics' and that Satan had no material power while, in the 'Age of Reason', the Royal Society looked upon witchcraft with some interest before declaring that there was no scientific (that is factual, and provable) evidence to suggest its existence.

So it was that in the late 17th century Robert Boyle summed up the position of many forward-thinking intellectuals nicely when he wrote: 'We live in an age and a place wherein all stories of witch-crafts or other magical feats are by many, even the wise, suspected; and by too many that would pass for wits derided and exploded.'

Other members of the Church of England who, by now, were no longer vying with Catholicism, saw witchcraft as a thing of the past; some of them questioning why the Devil would bother to prevent milk being churned into butter when the Great Plague of 1665-6 had killed 100,000 people in London alone ... surely this was more the Devil's work than any small domestic incident in a small town in Essex.

And so it was that in 1736 a new witchcraft Act was passed: 'An Act to repeal the Statute made in the First Year of the Reign of King James I; an Act against Conjuration, Witchcraft, and dealing with evil and wicked Spirits, except so much thereof as repeals an Act of the Fifth Year of the Reign of Queen Elizabeth, Against Conju-rations, Inchantments, and Witchcrafts, and to repeal an Act passed in the Parliament of Scotland in the Ninth Parliament of Queen Mary, intituled, Anentis Witchcrafts, and for punishing such Per-sons as pretend to exercise or use any kind of Witchcraft, Sorcery, Inchantment, or Conjuration.'

In short, from '24 June next ... Conjuration, Witchcraft, and deal-ing with evil and wicked Spirits, shall be repealed and utterly void, and of none effect.'

The Act went on to replace the crime of witchcraft with that of 'threats and fraud', especially when 'ignorant persons' were preyed upon; the punishment, by now, leading to at least a year's impris-onment (and every quarter the stocks) – bad enough, perhaps, but far healthier a punishment than 'examination' followed by death by hanging, fire, or by justice by water ...

Finally, in this chapter, while the 18th and 19th centuries saw a more measured, logical approach to so-called devilmongers or

**A witch? - No, Edmund Blampied's sketch of an old
Jersey woman peeling potatoes**

witchcraft, no laws and no church could destroy man's natural superstition … which is why we end Part I with a court case which
led to copious articles in the Evening Post in Jersey beginning in
September 1930 under the headline 'Alleged Black Magic' and
which centred on Cemetery Farm in St John, Jersey.

CHAPTER 6

AT the Police Court on Monday, 15 September 1930, Rollo Ahmed, aged 31, a native of Demerara, West Indies, and on remand, was charged with obtaining first £5, then £21.10s, (£21.50p) then £65 from Philip Dumaresq Rondel.

Two weeks later, on Saturday, 27 September 1930, a fuller account of Ahmed's alleged criminal activity was discussed during his trial. In court that day (Saturday Division) the Attorney-General charged that between 20 and 25 August Ahmed had 'criminally obtained' several sums of money by false pretence from Rondel by false pretences to which Ahmed's defence lawyer, Advocate Voisin, answered with a plea of not guilty.

After Ahmed's plea, he asked for bail on the grounds that his client's wife was pregnant. The appeal was refused and Ahmed was told that he would be sent for trial before the November Assizes.

So it was that Ahmed made a repeat appearance at court on Monday, 3 November, when he was accused of having criminally obtained £5 sterling, £21 10 shillings (50 pence) and £65 (13 banknotes of £5 each) between 20 and 25 August that year by false pretences from St John farmer Philip Dumaresq Rondel of Cemetery Farm, Vingtaine du Douet.

Through his counsel he again pleaded 'not guilty', although 20 witnesses would be called against him.

What was to follow showed that the Rondel household truly believed that all of their misfortunes had come about because they were bewitched; during the trial it emerged that six years earlier, in October 1924, Rondel had been sentenced to a month with hard labour for thumping a neighbour, Mr Hervieu, because he accused Hervieu of putting a spell on his farm and, in particular, on one of his horses.

Now, however, the tables were turned. It wasn't Rondel on trial but the West Indian Ahmed (31) who, the court was told, had asked for yet another £70 on 28 August 1930, explaining that the spirits who were destroying Rondel's farm were proving harder to remove than first envisaged.

Looking through the court records at the time it is obvious that Mrs Rondel was as superstitious as her husband but what, actually, had happened and what was to be the outcome of the trial?

As the events of those summer days in August 1930 unfolded, it appeared that Rondel bemoaned to his neighbours that both his crops and livestock were causing him great concern. He added that he believed it wasn't merely a case of bad luck; it was witchcraft. After that he was advised by his neighbour, Mr Alfred Ed. Surcouf, that 31-year-old Rollo Ahmed could help him – which he duly did, first asking for £5 and then even more as he told the farmer the spirits he was fighting against were proving more difficult to remove than he had first imagined.

Ahmed's fees continued to multiply, which in turn prompted Mrs Rondel to ask her father for £100 so that they could pay the accused and thus restore their farm to good health. So it was that she, and her father, Louis Jouanne, went to Lloyds and to banker J F Le Cornu to ask for the money; Mrs Rondel explaining that they needed it because they had had a bad potato season; one of their children was ill and that they were having trouble churning butter into milk.

The money was duly paid.

Meanwhile, Ahmed had 'purified' the house by going around it dressed in black robes and muttering a variety of incantations. He had also given Philip Rondel a ring to ward off evil spirits. Several packets of powder had also been sent to the farm on 7 August but, as the courts were told: 'The Rondels were afraid to open them as they were terrified that, if they did, that something terrible would happen to them.'

A fortnight later another package arrived, with an accompanying note demanding £70. If they did not pay, Ahmed wrote that 'something terrible' would happen to them. Accompanying the letter, which was sealed with the sign of a skull, signed 'Ahmed', was a matchbox containing a brown powder.

With some trepidation 'the witness opened it and touched it at Mrs Rondel's request, but neither she nor Mr Rondel, who fully expected to die after touching the powder, did so'.

Having been advised to go to law over what was, on the face of it, a simple matter of blackmail, the Rondels' case seemed water-tight, not least because the numbers of several of the £5 notes they had paid Ahmed had been recorded by the bank and at the post office so, when he tried to spend them, it was obvious that he was paying out money he had been given by Mr and Mrs Rondel.

However, a defiant Ahmed still tried to bluster his way through the courts, saying he had 'only ever been paid £5'; that he absolutely denied threatening the Rondels with death and that when he walked all through the farm with burning disinfectant and a knife he was merely 'fumigating the house' and not – as the Rondels had told the court – attempting to 'cut the throats of all the ghosts that lived therein'.

The black cloak he was accused of wearing, he said, never left his home ... it was for 'recreational use' only, and he could not account for the threatening letters being sent although, as the public prosecutor pointed out, each one labeled the address as 'Cemetry farm' (not 'Cemetery') ... and the accused was not renowned for his good use of written English.

Without doubt Ahmed was guilty but, before the Royal Court passed judgement, the Bailiff dismissed the idea that Ahmed was in touch with spirits. Instead, he said, he had preyed on the superstitions of a husband and wife whose farm was struggling to survive. Ahmed, he added, had been gifted the money through false pretences. It was as simple as that.

After his summing up, it took the jury a mere 16 minutes to find Ahmed guilty and he was duly sentenced to nine months' imprisonment with hard labour.

While Ahmed would rail against his sentence – why, the Rondels had approached him, he had never even thought to go to them! – it would have been no comfort to know that if his trial had been many years earlier he would have been 'hanged and strangled'. But the Rondels' initial faith in Ahmed's powers (Rondel even gave him a button from his shirt in the belief that it would help chase away the Devil, while Ahmed brought a doll into his house, to burn, and thus, he said, to destroy the evil spirits that lived in the farm) showed that while the courts dismissed witchcraft, as a crime, there was no way that they could undermine primitive beliefs.

If you were superstitious or if you believed in the supernatural, what physical laws could you write to guard yourself against your own imagination? – And the Rondels were not alone in the 20th century in being terribly afraid of Devilish powers for 'Satan' was to raise his ugly head more than once not 500 years ago but, on more than one occasion, in the 20th century including (again in Jersey) in 1954, when the Royal Court of Jersey couldn't decide whether the case against a Mr Thomas, initially tried for fraud, should, in fact, have been tried under the law concerning Divination because this crime had never been repealed.

Part 2
CHAPTER I

'A PURE FAITH'

AS we have seen, if the Channel Islands had remained a quiet, Catholic backwater, happy to pay their religious dues to the Bishop of Coutances, the great witch hunts of the 16th and 17th centuries would never have happened.

But they didn't – instead they allowed John Calvin's fierce, humourless Presbyterianism into Guernsey, Jersey and Sark, and alongside Calvinism came an obsessive terror of Satanism.

Calvin hated witchcraft as much as any Pope had ever done. He also mistrusted what he considered to be superstition and superstitious people, so any of his followers, arriving in the Channel Islands, would have been appalled at a so-called Christian society knee-deep in superstitious practices. As some Islanders quickly discovered, they were ill-equipped to cope with the severe discipline of Calvin-inspired ministers who expected them to attend church several times a week. There they would be told that the foolish pleasures they had been enjoying for years were godless, shameful and devilish. Who, though, at the beginning of the 16th century would have dared to predict that, in the space of a man's lifetime, such vehement piety would establish itself so deeply in Island society?

WHEN Henry VIII came to the throne in 1509 the great religious controversies of the 16th and 17th centuries were only faint wisps of cloud on the horizon. The immediate, day-to-day worries of the Islanders were more important, especially in outlying parishes, where farmers had to keep an eye out for marauding Frenchmen, or, in Jersey, a marauding Governor – Sir Hugh Vaughan.

Vaughan would just as soon rape a pretty girl as bid her 'good day' on his frequent rides through the countryside, and if the unfortunate girl sent her father to Mont Orgueil to complain, the father

'And there, tying their hands behind them by the two thumbs, drew them up to a certain height with an engine for that purpose, by which means sometimes their shoulders were turned round and sometimes their thumbs torn off ...'
(Beauregard Tower, Guernsey, arrowed)

would be beaten up or thrown into the cells by the Governor's men. Such acts went unpunished until 1532, when Sir Hugh was forced to resign. He took his pension book and new-found religious conscience back to England, where he became a regular, devout member of the local community.

Meanwhile, Islanders had to contend with the effect of continual attacks on their land, either from the French or from pirates or from the two together. As late as 1549 the French controlled Sark, using it as a handy naval base from which to attack the other islands or passing British ships. Lawlessness and injustice were no strangers to Islanders, which helps to explain their toleration of persecuted minorities who arrived on their shores seeking sanctuary.

Among those arriving in the Channel Islands, from France, not to pillage or spoil as the Vikings had done so many centuries before, were French Protestants or Presbyterians, for outlying Christian parishes were, for centuries, known as 'les presbytèries'. That the

'Perotine, who was great with child, did fall on her side where happened a ruefull sight; for as her belly burst asunder by the vehemence of the flames, the infant, being a fair man-child, fell into the fire'

these newcomers were prepared to die for their faith must have impressed the locals, particularly when the Catholic purge of Protestantism reached Normandy.

In 1528 a Protestant layman was burnt alive at Rouen, another at Coutances, and three women at Avranches. Technically, the first Protestants who arrived in Jersey were in as great a danger as they would have been if they had stayed in France, for the Islands were still part of the diocese of Coutances; although Henry VIII's decision to defy the Pope and marry Anne Boleyn seemed that their future was more secure.

Indeed, many Islanders had never been particularly fond of Catholicism because French monasteries owned good arable land in the Islands and there was a feeling that, if they were British, why should foreigners be allowed in to live off the fat of the land.

In 1536, when Henry VIII asked French priests living in the Channel Islands to swear an oath of allegiance to the English Crown instead of the Pope. Not unnaturally, they refused. Soon they were on their way back to their monasteries in Europe.

Edward VI then continued his father's policy of destroying the Islanders' allegiance to Rome. Priests were encouraged to renounce celibacy and marry local girls (which they did) while Catholic symbols, which at one time could be found at every crossroad, were destroyed or taken away and hidden. It would appear that nothing could stem this official anti-Catholic outburst: nothing, that is, until Mary I came to the throne in 1553.

Mary's five-year reign caused more agony that she would ever know, to newly married priests (who were thrown into prison, their marriage vows declared null and void), and to Catherine Cauchés and her two daughters, Guillemine Guilbert and Perotine Massey, who became pawns in the hands of their implacable Guernsey masters. They died because the Bailiff and the Dean (both Jerseymen) and certain jurats, in an attempt to convince their new Queen that they were, and always had been, convinced Catholics (their record until then had been decidedly shaky) decided to make a physical show of their enthusiasm for the faith.

They would destroy the women for heresy. Their trial and execution were blatantly unjust; none of the three was a heretic (far from it) and when they pleaded that their doctrine had been learnt at the time of Edward VI but, if the Queen was otherwise disposed 'they would be content with her religion', their cries were ignored. In John Fox's 'Book of Martyrs' we are given this account of their deaths: 'Then were three stakes set up. At the middle post was the mother, the eldest daughter on the right hand, the youngest on the other.

'They were first strangled, but the rope broke, before they were dead, and so the poor women fell on the fire. Perotine, who was great with child, did fall on her side, where happened a rueful sight; for, as her belly burst asunder by the vehemence of the flames, the infant, being a fair man-child, fell into the fire, and efstoons, being taken out of the fire by one W. House, was laid upon the grass.

'Then was the child had to the Provost, and from thence to the Bailiff, who gave censure that it should be carried back and cast into the fire.'

This ugly execution, meant to show Queen Mary that Guernsey was controlled by staunch Catholics, was a hollow victory and, if anything, stimulated Protestantism rather than destroyed it, especially when Queen Elizabeth I came to the throne in 1558.

One of her first acts was to remove the Bailiff, the Dean and the jurats from office. The jurats were then taken to London and fined, while Bailiff Helier Gosselin and Dean Jacques Amy were imprisoned for their part in the trial.

After craving the Queen's pardon far his 'erroneous judgement' Dean Amy was released. He returned to Guernsey and eventually became rector of St Saviour's parish before his death in 1586. Jacques Gosselin was released in 1565.

Within two years of the execution in Guernsey, Queen Elizabeth was on the throne and the Reformation continued at pace; Nicholas Baudain, an able minister from Rouen, established a church system based an the Presbyterian system in St Peter Port, while in St Helier, Jersey, Guillaume Morise of Anjou did the same.

Calvin would have been proud of the men, trying so hard to make their Islanders turn towards Protestantism. But it wasn't so easy, as Adrian de Saravia, Guernsey minister and schoolmaster, explained in a letter to Lord Cecil in 1565: 'If a minister goes into the country to preach, they greet him with laughter and jeers and sometimes the congregation makes such a noise that he is obliged to stop in his sermon, and, worse than this, they fill the pulpit with filth as well. They only keep their hands from actual violence from fear of the Queen's authority; if they were left to their own devices we should find them more barbarous than any Turks ...'

Left to their own devices, many Islanders would have preferred a more relaxed church (either Catholic or Protestant), or no church at all.

But it was not to be. Instead, after the massacre of Huguenots on St Bartholomew's Day in 1572 in France, Presbyterianism, based on Calvin's Geneva, was assured of a future in the Islands as a new wave of French refugees arrived here, many of them settling and

The scourge of Satan: Jean Calvin

becoming valuable members of the community and the local church. They might not always have been welcome – but they were safe.

Meanwhile, what was happening in Herm, Sark and Alderney?

Only Herm remained Catholic. The minister of Sark, Elie Brévint, refers to priests from Herm being seen in Jersey in 1619 and there is evidence to suggest that they were still living there some years later.

No Herm witches were ever brought to trial (which is hardly surprising, considering its small size and population) but local fishermen were convinced that on more than one occasion that witches could be seen rising over Herm, riding on their broomsticks in the general direction of Guernsey.

Sark, which was settled mainly by residents from St Ouen, Jersey, after the Seigneur of the parish, Helier de Carteret, had been issued with letters patent from Queen Elizabeth I allowing him to repopulate the island in 1565. He duly sent four suspected witches to Guernsey for trial, one of them (Rachel Alexandre) going to the stake on 10 August, 1627.

In view of the influence of the fiercely Presbyterian Brévint family, which provided ministers to Sark for over 100 years, it is surprising that more witches weren't sent to Guernsey for condemnation and punishment.

In Alderney, the third largest Island, there should have been fewer witches for, in 1584, the vaguely Catholic John Chamberlain was granted the island in fief by the Crown and, for 19 years, he was tenant, before being succeeded by his brother, William.

Because of their reluctance to have anything to do with Protestantism (even to the extent that they swallowed up all Church revenue for their own use) they protected the more eccentric of their subjects reasonably well from the other islands' Holy Synod.

Even so, four people living in Alderney were sent to Guernsey, accused of witchcraft, including Jean Béhot and Girette Parmentier, who, in 1620, were banished from the Channel Islands for life.

They could well have been accused because of their French origins (such outsiders were viewed with deep suspicion) but whether or not the same can be said of Jacob Gaudion we cannot say. He was banished for life in 1634. Five years late on 3 May, 1639, Emei Flères became the first, and last, Alderney resident to be burnt at the stake for sorcery.

CHAPTER 2

BETWEEN June, 1550 and October, 1661, at least 176 people appeared in Channel Island courts accused of sorcery. Of these, 36 Jersey and 46 Guernsey suspects were found guilty and executed. In Jersey the condemned man or woman was usually ordered to be taken from the courtroom 'with a rope around the neck to the place of execution to a post set up for that purpose'.

After the rope had been pulled tight and the victim was dead, the corpse was to be consumed by fire until it had been entirely reduced to ashes. The furniture and all assets of the dead 'witch' would then be confiscated, going to either the Crown or to the Seigneur in whose parish the deceased had lived.

Meanwhile, in Guernsey, the condemned man would have the long, winding walk from Beauregard Tower, down narrow steps to the Vallée de Misère (now La Charoterie, the Bordage and Fountain Street). There he would be greeted by a large crowd (executions were open to the public) and hoisted onto a gibbet, above brushwood. As the wood was fired it was sometimes debatable which had taken the man's life first – the flame or the rope around his neck. Either way, it was good free entertainment for the large crowds. As in Jersey, after the body had been reduced to ashes these would be scattered and any possessions the witch had would revert to the Crown.

OTHER men were responsible for condemning so many Islanders, branding them as witches, but no man's influence was greater than one who was not an Islander, John Calvin.

Calvin (in French, Cauvin), logical, argumentative, was a man incapable of compromise whose personality and sense of grim religious devotion appealed to so many Island leaders over the years. Born in 1504 and converted to Luther's beliefs in 1534, he was a man who devised a system of religious administration every bit as authoritative as Catholicism but a good deal less picturesque.

Calvin was a superb administrator as well as a fervent preacher, who taught that God, offended by Adam's rebellious nature, was

**Steps leading down to the Vallée Misère (Vale of Misery) from
Beauregard Tower, Guernsey. The condemned prisoners
walked down here to the stake, set up near the market place**

exacting a terrible vengeance on mankind which could only be
avoided by a strictly imposed discipline – so who better to discipline the exponents of original sin than his own Church of the
Elect?

His Church of the Elect, however, wasn't something you just
joined. God 'called' His followers to Him, and whenever the Elect
were convinced that they had been summoned and that Christ was
at one with them, then here was a cell of the true Calvinist Church.
The idea that Christ's presence could be felt close at hand was very
dear to Calvin and, if His presence could be felt, then so, too, could

Satan's. For if anyone stumbled along the Christian path, the Devil was always willing to buy, beg or steal another lapsed Soul.

If Calvin had had a sense of humour or had been capable of a few self-doubts, fewer people might have suffered in God's name. Instead he devised a religious system which, once it dominated a community, did so with a sense of righteousness that it was impossible to argue against.

The system was layered; the congregation created Elders, Pastors, and Teachers, whose parish assembly was called a consistory, their Island assembly was called a colloquy and, if members of the colloquy were also members of the States Assembly (the Island government), it meant that a handful of people had control over both spiritual and workaday life.

Some Islanders must have enjoyed great satisfaction knowing how much power they had over their fellow Islanders – but this was at the upper level of the hierarchical pyramid.

At the lower level were those people who just wanted to get on with the everyday, ordinary business of life without any fuss. Unfortunately they weren't allowed to do so for their Elders (and Pastors and Teachers) knew better than they.

As religious fever raged in the hearts and minds of some of the most influential Islanders, this meant it was inevitable that anyone not so committed ran the risk of being labelled a non-believer. Yet piety, for some, must have been a terrible bind. Their whole lives were controlled by prayer.

The same was true in certain households in England and to give an idea of the kind of life that an Islander was expected to lead what follows is an extract from Lady Margaret Hoby of Hackness's diary, dated Friday, 21 December 1599.

'After a privat praier I ded a little, and so went to church: after the sermon I praied, then dined, and, in the afternone, was busy tell five o'clock; then I returned to privat praier and examenation; after supped, then hard publeck praiers and, after that, praied privatly, having reed a Chapter of the Bible, and so went to bed.'

This was only a weekday. On a Sunday the routine of prayer would have been more rigorous. A similar attitude to life was expected in Jersey, Guernsey and Sark.

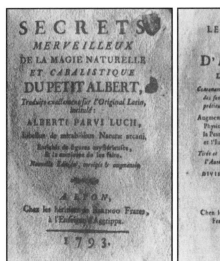
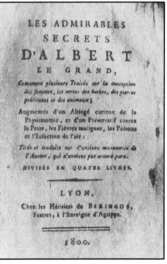

Two of the most important 'grimoires' or 'Devil books', both of which were well-known in the Islands: 'le p'tit Albaert' and 'le grand Albaert'

Islanders were expected to attend church twice on Sunday and there was a catechism for children in the afternoon. There were weekday services, at which one person 'able to hear and understand' the service was required to be present and, if no-one did attend, the head of the household could be punished.

Communion services were held once a quarter and everyone over the age of 12 who did not attend risked a morning (or more) in the stocks. Afternoons were given to learning the catechism and the more devoted Presbyterians knew by heart the 400 responses to the handbook which defined an Islander's creed.

If you faltered along the Christian path reprisals or, as the Elders saw it, Christian justice, was inevitable. Elders could enforce moral as well as spiritual discipline and were empowered to: 'Watch over the life and morals of the flock, to reprove slight failings by the Word of God, and to report more serious ones to the consistory.'

Elders, like some kind of plain-clothes policemen, were expected to question parishioners about the moral character of their neighbours and any scandal, real or imaginary, had to be reported back to the consistory.

Penalties incurred by recalcitrant church-goers varied. For a minor offence a parishioner would be taken bareheaded and bare-footed to a penitent's bench where, dressed in a white sheet and looking suitably humble, he would be expected to confess his faults with a burning torch in one hand, a Bible in the other.

Meanwhile, the minister would deliver a scathing sermon, detailing every sin the offender had committed. For a more serious offence the threat of excommunication was ever-present. And, if a parishioner was unfortunate enough to be disowned by the Church, then he or she might just as well turn to the Devil, for mercy was very difficult to obtain and 'being cut off as a septic limb from the body of Christ, as Adam was expelled from Paradise by a flaming sword' was the first step along the road to Hell.

To add to the misfortunes of irreligious Islanders, the ecclesiastical courts were given full support by civil authorities.

Calvin, in Geneva, had encouraged Christians to take an active part in government and the Channel Islands' 1576 'Police and Discipline' document prepared by the Holy Synod urged that Church members involve themselves in political life. They did so, and many Church Elders were also jurats and local government officials centrally or at parish level. They made certain that legislation was passed to strengthen the moral character of the Islanders, whether they wanted it strengthening or not.

Swearing became a fineable offence, dancing, skittle-playing or gossiping on a Sunday were forbidden and, in 1558, the Royal Court of Jersey ordered that anyone found attending an all-night party and singing 'lascivious songs or telling licentious stories' would be fined 20 sols.

It must have been a horribly repressive world for anyone wanting a bit of fun for there was always the feeling that if you did enjoy yourself too much, it was because the Devil had entered your soul. Under such a rigorous Christian regime the idea that Satan lived, walked abroad and breathed on your windows was very real and if memories of old pagan gods had faded, the character of the Islanders was still the same. There was natural appeal in the idea that somewhere, wandering the narrow country lanes, was a cloven-footed gentleman, ready to tempt anyone who crossed his path. In the outlying parishes in particular people began to look out for signs that the Devil was there, and if you look for something hard enough, it isn't difficult to find.

So cattle which didn't give milk were said to have been touched by the Devil, milk that didn't turn to butter had been looked at by the Devil (or by one of his disciples) and, with the full blessing of the Church, Islanders were encouraged to take an unhealthy interest in their neighbours' behaviour.

In a paradoxical way this meant that superstition was being encouraged, not destroyed, for church-going parishioners (still extremely superstitious themselves) were being encouraged to look for signs of Devilry in their equally superstitious neighbours.

Eventually, of course, Satanists, witches, devilmongers – call them what you will – were found, including some who had strayed from the straight and narrow in remarkable fashion, especially those who believed that the Devil's blood had been in their family for generations or that they had been conceived under a moonlit sky during a midnight Sabbat.

But there were also the others – people who weren't so much evil as weak-willed, people who were lusty and immoral, who slept with their husband's brothers or who got drunk and fell into a ditch once too often. And then there were the muddle-headed, the old and the crotchety, people who paid for their eccentricity with their lives.

More than one little old woman, who had never belonged to a convent but who may have been a little strange in her life-style, must have ended her days by walking down those narrow steps from Beauregard Tower, to the Vallée de Misère, unsure of what she had done wrong and why she was there, but knowing that she was making a one-way trip to nowhere.

The gibbets and the brushwood were waiting.

CHAPTER 3

CATHOLICS and Calvin – the two blended no better than oil and water yet, despite their differences, there were similarities, including a hatred of anything that smelt of the Devil and a liking for books which explained how to deal with devilmongers once they were caught.

In the 16th century when Calvin was at the peak of his power and after moveable type had been invented it was possible to obtain mass-produced books, many of them written to serve as another weapon in the Christian artillery directed against evil.

However, if books could be written to attack Devilish practices, they could also be written by people keen to promote them. In effect during the 16th and 17th centuries there was a war of words ... Devil books versus the rest. The profane works included grimoires, textbooks on magic which typically included instructions on how to create magical objects such as talismans and amulets, how to perform magical spells, charms and divination and also how to summon or invoke supernatural entities such as angels, spirits, and demons.

Even the books themselves were believed to be imbued with magical powers, both good and bad, and as recently as the late 1980s staff at the Priaulx Library in Guernsey refused to touch them. In theory, of course, grimoires, like books which tell you how to manufacture a H- bomb, are not dangerous per se. It is the information they contain and how that information is used which threatens society.

Bought at either the Guibray or Lessay fairs in Normandy, the grimoires would be brought to the Islands and their information be passed on by word of mouth ... and pretty odd pieces of information they might well be, too.

Nowadays we might smile at some of the hocus-pocus nonsense the books contain and the two most popular in the Islands, 'Le Grand Albaert' and 'Le p'tit Albaert' (collectively known as 'The Marvelous Secrets of Albert the Great') contain more bizarre information than most. Based on the studies into mystery and magic by the 13th century bishop of Ratisbon, the books had appeared in a French translation by 1538, and, as well as telling their readers how to hypnotise a horse, they gave some quite disgusting medical advice, including a method of abortion which would terrify any modern-day would-be mother.

However, their effect on our ancestors must have been profound, with an assortment of legends entwining themselves around the books, some of which are believed today.

For example, even now if you pay money for a grimoire you may well be selling part of your soul, and once you have bought one of the wretched things, it is impossible to get rid of it, try as you might. No matter how deep you bury it, or how far you fling it out to sea, allegedly it will reappear on your bookcase as good as new. Trying to destroy it by fire is also pointless for, Phoenix-like, it can rise from the ashes.

The only tried and tested way of ensuring that it will never return is to take it to consecrated ground, sprinkle holy water over it and say a few prayers before burying it deep into the ground. Then, once you arrive home, you have to keep your fingers crossed in the hope that no-one will ever disturb it, for grimoires, it is said, don't fade with age or decompose like any mortal book.

And depending on the strength of your faith, they can bring you exceedingly bad fortune. One Guernsey farmer, for example, blamed his daughter's death and his own unhappiness on having introduced them into his house.

However, it isn't the legends associated with the grimoires nor the quack remedies which alarmed our Christian fathers to the greatest extent; instead it was the advice they contained relating to conjuring (the word used to describe how spirits can be summoned from another world) which alarmed them most.

In the 'Marvelous Secrets' advice is given explaining how it is possible to reach out and use dark powers of the Unknown, and in the 'Key of Solomon' ('Clavicula Salomonia'), perhaps the most famous Devil book of all time, the formula for raising spirits is given in full and elaborate diagrams and warnings are included to ensure that nothing goes wrong. Apparently a word or symbol out of place and instead of controlling the spirit, the conjuror will allow himself to be controlled in turn, with the unhealthy prospect that his mind and body will be ripped to pieces by the untamed spirit.

Why anyone should want to summon such a beast, knowing that it might rip your mind apart is another matter, but grimoires do contain such terrible information and, in an age of iPods and e-mails can still be found in Island homes to this day.

IRONICALLY, a book which was written to curb the activities of people who might well buy grimoires, the 'Malleus Maleficarum', which has already been mentioned, (the 'Hammer of the Witches') had a crueller, more evil streak than the nastiest of grimoires. Its influence on Europe and in the Channel Islands was devastating. As mentioned previously, it was written by Dominican fathers Heinrich Kramer and Jacob Sprenger in 1484, after which it became a sort of do-it-yourself guide to witch-hunting. By 1520, with Pope Innocent VIII's anti-heretic and anti-witch Bull 'Summus Desiderantes Affectibus' (which made special mention of intercourse with 'Demons, Incubi and Succubi') as preface, it had been reprinted 14 times, and was used by Catholic and Protestant alike, with no-one keener in its use then Martin Luther, who told his followers that witches were an important battalion in the vast legion of enemies that the Devil was assembling against the true Church.

It was also popular with Calvin and became a model for many other similar text books, invaluable in witch trials when neither the inquisitor nor the accused was really sure what was expected of them. In hindsight, Kramer and Sprenger have a lot to answer for, but let us briefly flick through the pages: 'Women are naturally more impressionable ... They have slippery tongues, and are unable to conceal from their fellow women those things which by evil arts they know ... Women are intellectually the children ... (Woman) is more carnal than a man, as is clear from her many carnal abominations ... She is an imperfect animal, she always deceives ... Therefore a wicked woman is by her nature quicker to waver in her faith, and consequently quicker to objure the faith, which is the root of witchcraft ...'

Having condemned women out of hand, the book explains in greater detail the four essential points of witchcraft: renunciation

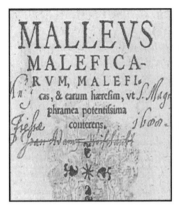

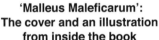

'Malleus Maleficarum':
The cover and an illustration
from inside the book

of the Catholic faith; devotion of body and soul to the services of evil; offering up unbaptised children to the Devil; engaging in orgies which included intercourse with Satan. Witches were also able to change shape, fly through the air and bring illness to their neighbours, and such was their cunning that it was virtually impossible to discover who they were. The Devil's children could destroy a community while all the time suggesting that they were sweetness and light, so it was best to suspect everyone and to trust no-one until a Christian court had arrived at its verdict.

With the terrible principle that you are guilty until proved innocent, the 'Malleus Maleficarum' advocated brutal torture to extract confessions from suspects on the premise that, with the Devil's help, one of his disciples could tolerate a terrible amount of pain before admitting his or her guilt.

So once you were arrested and suspected of being a witch you might never see daylight again. The jailer's task was to prove you guilty by all the means at his disposal and these included bone-crushers, the rack and, in Guernsey, a machine which held you firm while it kept turning – the strappado: 'The custom then was, when any person was supposed guilty of sorcery or witchcraft, they carried them to a place in the town called "La Tour Beauregard" and there, tying their hands behind them by the thumbs, drew them to a certain height with an engine made for that purpose, by which means sometimes their shoulders were turned round, and sometimes their thumbs torn off.'

As your body was being pulled apart in such a way that the temptation to admit to a crime, any crime, must have been overwhelming. More than one Guernsey 'witch' was condemned by her own mouth, simply because she couldn't bear any further punishment.

Sadly, once she (almost invariably a 'she') had admitted her guilt the ordeal was not yet over. Before being taken out and burnt at the stake a condemned witch would often be tortured again, to make her realise the enormity of her crime and to persuade her to reveal the names of her fellow Satanists.

No wonder that so-called friends of an accused person would often be the first to offer evidence against her, realising that if they didn't speak out first then the so-called witch might be tempted to accuse them of being her accomplices, just to gain a brief respite from the torment she was going through.

Yes, Kramer and Sprenger have a lot to answer for, but their influence could not have been so great if other people were not terrified of the real threat of Devilmongery, on a universal scale. That fear was common to the Papacy and to Protestants and in England King James I was so worried by witchcraft that he produced his own anti-witch book in 1597, before he came to the throne, called 'Daemonologie'. In the book James proclaimed that anyone who did not believe in the Christian faith was liable to be 'given over in the hands of the Devil, that enemy, to beare his Image, and thus take pleasure in the grossest impietie.'

With literature like this and the 'Malleus Maleficarum' in their hands and with Christian and royal authority behind them, witchhunters throughout Europe as well as the UK were in a position of overwhelming strength.

They frequently knew more about witchcraft than the people they were arresting, which would have been small comfort to an innocent suspect like Burgomaster Junius of Bamberg. A letter, dated 24 July, 1628, and smuggled out of jail to his daughter, reads as follows: 'Many hundred thousand good-nights, dearly beloved daughter Veronica. Innocent have I come to prison, innocent have I been tortured, innocent must I die. For whoever comes into the witch prison must become a witch or be tortured until he invents something out of his head and – God pity him, bethinks of something. I will tell you how it has gone with me ...

'And then came the executioner, and put the thumbscrews on me, so that the blood ran out of the nails and everywhere, so that for four weeks I could not use my hands as you see from the writing ...

'Thereafter they first stripped me, bound my hands behind me, and drew me up in torture...

'Then I thought Heaven and Earth were at an end; eight times did they draw me up and let me fall again, so that I suffered terrible agony.

'The executioner said: "Sir, I beg you, for God's sake, confess something, whether it be true or not, for you cannot endure the torture which you will be put to, and even if you bear it all, yet you will not escape ...".'

(The Burgomaster begged a day to think, invented a story of a witch's meeting while, under the threat of further torture, named several people as sorcerers).

The letter continues: 'Now, dear child, here you have all my confession, for which I must die. And they are sheer lies and made-up things, so help me God. For all this I was forced to say through fear of the torture which was threatened beyond what I had already endured. For they never leave off with the torture till one confesses something; be he never so good, he must be a witch. Nobody escapes, though he were an earl ...

'Dear child, keep this letter secret so that people do not find it, else I shall be tortured most piteously, and the jailers will be beheaded. So strictly is it forbidden ... Dear child, pay this man a dollar ... I have taken several days to write this; my hands are both lame. I am in a sad plight. Good night, for your father Johannes Junius will never see you more.'

(In the margin was written 'Dear child, six have confessed against me at once; the Chancellor, his son ... all false, through compulsion, as they have told me, and begged my forgiveness in God's name before they were executed.')

A few months later in Guernsey, in May 1629, Marguerite Picot was suffering a similar ordeal. She was eventually burnt at the stake that year, but the cruellest time for Guernsey witches was 1617, when seven Islanders enjoyed a one-way conversation with the local executioner.

As in Europe, when a suspect was arrested in the Island, he or she was presumed guilty until they could prove their innocence the best way possible.

It was not an easy thing to do and the way you were questioned allowed little room for manoeuvre. 'How old were you when the Devil first appeared to you? Why did you choose to become a witch? Who are the children on whom you have cast a spell? When did you first attend the Sabbat? Which demon did you choose to be your lover?'

It was virtually impossible to defend yourself against questions meant to confirm guilt, rather than to deny it. It was also extremely difficult to answer sensibly when your body was being pulled apart and, if a suspect did manage to hold out for any length of time, there were other ways of proving guilt which didn't involve question-and-answer sessions.

The inquisitor, for example, would search for the Devil's mark (either a small blue tattoo or an insensitive piece of skin), the searching being done with a long pin, which was pricked into all parts of the body. When no blood was drawn or when the victim didn't appear to be in pain the court were informed that the 'mark' had been found. Or, a Devil's 'pap' might be discovered – a third teat supposedly used to suckle a Devil's familiar. Cats, toads and crows were the usual familiars, supposedly acting as intermediaries between the Devil and his disciple.

While no Channel Islanders were ever 'ducked' in water to find out whether or not they were witches, as happened in Britain, once they had been found guilty and executed it was important that their ashes were scattered to the four winds, as was the European tradition, for the courts and most God-fearing Islanders were genuinely concerned in case there was some kind of miraculous rebirth and the accused would come back to haunt them.

Such concern was genuine, for didn't the Bible say: '*A man also*

During the trials in Guernsey, the greffier who wrote up the court's sentence would doodle alongside it his own version of what would happen to each convicted 'witch'

a woman that hath a familiar spirit or that is a wizard, shall surely be put to death: they shall stone them with stones; their blood shall be upon them.'

(King James' Bible, 1611: Leviticus 20.27).

IF the Bible condemned sorcery, so did the government. Remembering the treatment of the Burgomaster of Bamberg, below is a confession of Isabel Becquet, who was burned as a witch on 4 July 1617, at the Vallée de Misère, in Guernsey. Hers is a poignant story, highlighted by the pauses in this story which are pin-pointed by three dots. These correspond to similar pauses in the original records, which, so it is said, were fleeting moments as the jailer relaxed his brutal interrogation, so allowing his victim a chance to speak.

'Isabel, wife of Jean le Moygne, having been put to the question at once confessed that she was a witch ... and that upon getting into a quarrel with the woman Girarde, who was her sister-in-law ... the

Devil, in the form of a hare, took occasion to tempt her ... appearing to her in broad daylight in a road near her house ... and persuading and inciting her to give herself to him ... and that he would help to avenge herself on the said Girarde, and everybody else ... to which persuasion she would not at the moment condescend to yield ... so he at once disappeared ... but very soon he came again to her in the same road, and pursuing his previous argument ... exhorted her in the same terms as above ... that done, he left her and went away, after having previously put her a sackful of parsnips; she then took a certain black powder wrapped in a cloth which he placed; which powder she kept by her.

'He appeared to her another time under the same form in the town district, inciting her anew to give herself to him but she, not wishing to comply, he next made a request to her to give him some living animal ... whereupon she returned to her dwelling and fetched a chicken, which she carried to him to the same place where she had left him, and he took it ... and after having thanked her he made an appointment for her to be present the next morning before daylight at the Sabbath, promising that he would send for her ... according to which promise, during the ensuring night, the old woman, Collette du Mont, came to fetch her, and gave her some black ointment, which she had had from the Devil; with this (after having stripped herself) she anointed her back and belly, then having dressed herself again she went out of the house door ... when she was instantly caught up ... and carried across hedges and bushes to the banks of the seashore, in the neighbourhood of Rocquaine Castle, the usual place where the Devil kept his Sabbath ... no sooner had she arrived there than the Devil came to her in the form of a dog, with two great horns sticking up ... and with one of his paws (which seemed to her like hands) took her by the hand ... and calling her by her name told her that she was welcome.'

From our perpective in the 21st century, this all sounds like nonsense, but we must remember that in the 16th and 17th centuries such confessions would, by many, be taken literally.

CHAPTER 4

THE WITCH TRIALS

WITCHES: they appeared in the courts in all shapes and sizes, from all walks of life, adopting all sorts of attitudes and, eventually, many of them confessed to their crimes. Many of those confessions would not have been given willingly, although more than a few people openly admitted that they had seen the Devil; that they had enjoyed intercourse with him; that they had the power to cast the 'evil eye' on their neighbours and on their neighbours' cattle.

Sometimes these confessions were little more than shows of foolish bravado – they were going to die, so why not go down fighting? – but this was not always the case. There were, indeed, some people alive at the time, who, legend has it, went to La Rocqueberg in Jersey, or Le Catioroc in Guernsey and danced themselves into a frenzy before copulating with each other or with a shadowy black figure who played the part of 'Le Tchéziot' (the Devil).

Pasquette Le Vésconte, for example, who had 'previously been arrested for witchcraft and banished for ever from the Island (Jersey) but had returned contrary to the said sentence, and continued to use diabolical devices and spells' may well have been to a Sabbat at La Rocqueberg.

In December 1585, she was arrested for a second time for 'malléfices diaboliques', confessed that she had entered into partnership with the Devil and 'by his help had perpetrated innumerable crimes and homicides'. She was accordingly executed.

Jean Morant, also from Jersey, and a native of St Clement, admitted his dealings with the Devil and confessed: '... son accointance avec le diable par merche et promesse confermée soubz gage et don de l'ung de ses membres ...' (he had sacrificed a knuckle in homage to his master).

However, if Le Vésconte and Morant had been evil, at least they had not been born to their evil ways – unlike Marie Tourgis. Her whole family seem to have had devilish connections. There is an old Jersey saying which runs: 'Si tais si maychante, j'enviethai cherchi Marie Tourgis.' ('If you're such a bad girl, I'll send for Marie Tourgis'.)

The words would send children scurrying home before night or keep them huddled under the blankets, afraid to peep out in case the evil witch of Grouville was looking at them. According to the records, however, Marie's mother was just as evil. In October, 1608, Andrée Tourgis was arrested for sorcery. In the course of her trial she admitted that she had killed her grand-daughter, her daughter Mabel's child. For this, on 13 October, she was sentenced to be hanged. On the same day her other daughters, Marie and Jeanne, were put on trial charged with crimes connected with sorcery.

Neither girl was very old at the time and they were released on the understanding that they would change their way of life.

Marie was discharged into the care of a God-fearing family, but she seems to have been incapable of giving up her previous bad habits. Ten years later she was on trial again.

Having confessed that she had caused the death of a child and had bewitched a woman so completely that she was 'afraid for her life', Marie was convicted of *'la crime diabolique de sortilège'* and, nearly ten years to the day after her mother had been executed she, too, was taken out to the market place and hanged.

Her sister, Jeanne, was to live for some years longer, but not in Jersey, for in February 1613, she was found guilty of associating with witches and was banished: such a relatively lenient sentence spared Jeanne's life, but by this time members of the Tourgis family in Guernsey were also finding it difficult to adjust to a Christian regime. On 17 October 1622, Thomas Tourgis of the Forest and his daughter, Jeanne, were burnt at the stake on the outskirts of St Peter Port for their involvement with witchcraft. We do not know whether they were related to the Tourgis family from Jersey.

While the Bailiffs and jurats of the two main islands were trying their hardest to prevent the influence of the Tourgis families from spreading, they were equally concerned about the Grandin family (in Jersey) and the Becquet family (in Guernsey).

In 1597 Phillipe Grandin had been hanged for theft. In 1606, Marie and Elizabeth Grandin, quite young girls, were arrested for sorcery and warned 'not to gad about the Island, nor to threaten to speak evil of anyone, under pain of being rearrested and punished for the crime with which they had been charged'.

The Bailiffs also ordered them to 'walk in the fear of God, to attend Divine service regularly, to live in peace and concord with their neighbours' and to be better behaved and more virtuous in the future. Perhaps they did try hard to mend their ways but it was difficult to do so when other relatives were so obviously such a bad influence. In 1618, for example, Barthelmy Grandin was hanged for larceny and in 1631 Jeanne Grandin was hanged and burnt for sorcery.

In 1648, 42 years after her first trial, Elizabeth was rearrested. She was accused of 'living a lewd, wicked and scandalous life' and she and her daughter, Marie, also on trial, were lucky to escape with a warning. Not so lucky was another Grandin, also called Marie, who lived in Trinity. She was accused of 'having by diabolical spells caused many persons to die, and others to fall into decline, and also much cattle (to do the same)'.

Although she denied her guilt to the bitter end, after 70 witnesses had spoken against her she was taken, struggling, to the stake. Afterwards her body was burnt and the ashes scattered to the winds.

The Tourgis family and the Grandin family had (or so it was alleged) bad blood in them. But so did Guernsey's Becquet family and if anyone was foolish enough to become involved with them (particularly with Collas Becquet) they did so at their own risk.

Most Islanders knew of these families' reputations and tried to keep out of their way or, if any of them came begging, they made certain that they gave something substantial in case the 'evil eye' was cast upon them.

It was believed that a witch could give or take life depending on the strength of his (or her) will so, not unnaturally, it was thought best to avoid a witch placing a spell on you.

Repeatedly in the court records in both Guernsey and Jersey witnesses speak of being infested or tormented after a witch's spell had been discovered in bed. Nowadays we think of spells being some kind of magical incantation but 16th century spells were not always mere words; they could be objects made of hempen thread, twisted with feathers and bound together by clay and excreta. Some

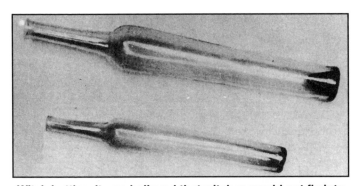

Witch bottles. It was believed that witches would not fly into your room at night if you placed them in the rafters. The bottles might be filled with holy water or urine as a deterrent

spells would be round, like apples, others would be flat, like the palm of the hand; all would be cursed and placed as near as possible to the victim. They were also called 'sorcerots' and one of their alleged powers was to introduce vermin into victims' homes.

The spells that were placed in Pierre Rougier's house, however, were not meant to introduce lice or fleas. They were there to destroy him – or so his wife, Susanne, believed. In her deposition against Collas Becquet dated 17 May 1617, she describes how Pierre had been in agony for 12 days before dying and she was certain that one of the causes for her husband's death had been the spells that had been placed in his bed. She also told of finding 44 spells in her child's bed. She was certain Collas was doing her family harm.

Many other Guernsey people were terrified of Becquet, who obviously enjoyed his evil reputation. Included in these was Collas Hughes, who had been to a wedding earlier that year. Becquet was also invited. 'Collas Becquet arrived there, and began to toy with his (Hughes') daughter-in-law, who repelled his advances; the very same evening she was taken ill in such a manner that they thought she would have died from one hour to another; besides which she remained under the charm, and they found one of the witch's spells in her bed, which was shown to the Members of the Court, who were making an inspection at St Peter's; the said girl sometimes fell to the ground quite blinded.'

Another witness was Thomas Brouart. He told the court that Becquet had placed a curse on his bed and his clothing in such a way that his blankets were filled with so many maggots that they resembled an ant-hill, and a brand-new vest Brouart had bought was so covered by lice that it was impossible to see the cloth beneath.

Brouart's guardian, Thomas de Lisle, threw the infested garment into a cabbage patch and sought out the wife of one of Becquet's friends, threatening to beat her up unless all the vermin were removed. On his return the vest lay vermin-free among the cabbages.

In all, 171 witnesses testified against CoIlas Becquet. They would not all have been simple-minded or thirsting for revenge – Becquet, if not a Satanist, was an unpleasant man, apparently with alarming powers.

Other members of the Becquet family were also arrested. Five, in all, were tried for witchcraft, and we know that at least two of these were devoured by flames and that one was banished from the Island. It did not pay to be friendly with the Becquet family, either, as the Massis discovered to their cost. They knew them well and three of them paid for their friendship with their lives.

Anne and her son Pierre were burnt at the stake and younger son, Jéhan Massi, was put on trial; what happened to him we don't know, as the Court's decision has not been recorded. Pierre Massi (senior) was sentenced to be burnt at the stake but on 1 May 1619 he escaped from custody and suffered a fate which has more than a touch of grim irony about it. He was swept out to sea and drowned, which should have proved his innocence – if it's true that witches float on water.

An unenlightened Guernsey Court, however, insisted that his guilt remained even after his death. If the Massi family were evil, as the Becquets were thought to be evil, perhaps they deserved their fate. Yet there is an irony, for in the official records we read: '4 July 1617. Collette du Mont, widow of Jean Becquet, Marie, her daughter, wife of Pierre Massy and Isabel Becquet, wife of Jean Le Moygne ... *voluntarily submitted themselves* to the courts being by common rumour and report for a long time past addicted to the damnable art of witchcraft.'

They were apprehended by the officers of his Majesty King James I before many of their neighbours spoke against them. The officers then told the court that 'it was clear and evident that for many years past the(se) women had practised the diabolical art of witchcraft by having not only cast their spells upon inanimate objects but also by having retained in languor through strange diseases many persons and beasts; and also cruelly hurt a great number of men, women and children and caused the death of many animals ... Also (that) according to the deposition given by Isabel Becquet, members of both families attended the Sabbat.'

Having tried to prove (and failed) that these women were part of a 13-women coven, His Majesty's officers had to content themselves with taking 'said women' with halters about their necks to 'the usual place of punishment' where they were fastened by the Executioner to the gallows before being hanged, strangled, killed and burnt until their flesh and bones were reduced to ashes, the ashes then scattered before all their goods, chattels and estates were forfeited to His Majesty.'

IF the Guernsey records are accurate, the period between 1610 and 1630 was a particularly virulent one for black magic in the Island. In all 59 people were tried *'d'avoir practiquée de long main l'horrible et enormé crime de sorcellerie.'*

In Jersey, witch trials reached their grisly climax between 1585 and 1625. Five people were sentenced in 1585, another five in 1591, three each in 1599 and 1600, five in 1625.

As in Guernsey most crimes connected with sorcery included the killing and maiming of animals – a serious offence in an age when livestock was the most valuable possession a family might have; the use of different powders to sour a neighbour's milk or turn it into blood; plus the 'crime' of allowing sheep or cattle to stray into other fields (which Elizabeth Grandin had been seen doing).

It seems reasonable to assume that if some of these witches hadn't been tried for sorcery they would have been tried and executed for other crimes. Threats, abuse, destruction of property, bullying – all were part and parcel to the way that a Tourgis or Grandin lived his or her life.

Sexual crimes, too, were commonplace. Whether at the Sabbat

or next door in a neighbour's house, according to the Bible it was still wrong to covet someone else's wife or husband. Court records in Jersey for 24 May 1648 read: 'Guillemette du Vaistain, native of parts of Normandy, was brought to the court by the constable and officers of the parish of St Ouen for crimes of devil-worship and sorcery and for having refused on many occasions to submit to the inquest of the land (and) who freely admitted to having had carnal copulation with one of her brothers-in-law.'

The court believed that Guillemette was guilty and, because of the seriousness of the crime, she was ordered to be 'punished with the whip at the hands of the executioner' and that she 'should be soundly lashed at the doorway of the court of justice, in the open air, until blood was drawn and, like a useless member, wicked and unacceptable, she should then be banished for ever from the Island, forbidden to return under pain of death'.

Furthermore, all of her belongings were to be confiscated and presented to the King or Seigneur of her parish. (In May 1648 Guillemette was well into middle age).

Sadly, even helpful sorcery was not to be trusted and when a mother or father, desperate for a cure for a child's illness went to a white witch for help – still commonplace in many peasant communities – the courts were quick to intervene.

In October 1585, Jacques Le Brocq's daughter fell ill, so two of the family consulted a woman who, it was rumoured, practised witchcraft. For this the father was put on trial for allowing 'improper steps' to be used in healing his daughter and, having been found guilty, Mathieu and Jean le Brocq were committed for a short while to the castle at Mont Orgueil.

In 1591 the Royal Court was so upset by the number of Islanders who were visiting sorcerers it issued the following proclamation: 'Whereas many have in days gone by committed the heinous sin of seeking aid in time of trouble from warlocks and witches, a thing contrary to the honour of God and His express command, and a grievous insult to the Christian faith, and to those whose duty it is to administer Justice; and whereas Ignorance is no excuse for Sin, and no-one can tell what depravity may ensue from such practices; in order that henceforth all may turn from these wicked and devilish cures, the use of which merits by God's Law the same penalty as is inflicted on warlocks and witches themselves, and that God's wrath may be averted, which now threatens the Officers of Justice, because of the impunity with which these crimes are committed; all who dwell in this Island are strictly forbidden to receive aid or advice in trouble from warlocks or witches or anyone suspected of witchcraft under pain of a month's imprisonment in the Castle on dry bread and water, with the reservation that they must declare in Court their excuse for such effrontery, and according as this shall appear reasonable, be dealt with as God's Law directs.'

23 December, 1591

GUERNSEY also warned Islanders about the dangers of going to a sorcerer for advice and, of course, they offered the ultimate deterrent to anyone foolish enough to dabble in witchcraft – death; and, while English courts saw witchcraft as a civil offence and never officially sentenced witches to be burnt at the stake, Guernsey continued to hang, strangle and burn them until 1639.

Although the punishment has no element of humour in it at all, the greffier (chief clerk) of the day, whose task it was to record the sentencing of the condemned witches, seems to have had macabre fascination with the Bailiff's summing up. As we have seen, in the margin of the official court records of the trials he has sketched childish cartoons of men and women tied to a post, or hanging from the gallows, while below flames are leaping at their feet.

While the greffier was intrigued by the fate of prisoners as they listened to the Bailiff pronounce sentence, so were the public. In the main islands a public execution was treated as if a carnival had come to town and you had to arrive early if you wanted a good view.

Witch-burning must have been especially popular, for there was always the slight possibility that if Satan was going to intervene at the last moment and whisk his disciple out of the flames.

It never happened, although Sir Edgar McCulloch relates one occasion when only the bravery of warder Gosselin prevented a devilish escape. 'About the year 1640 there happened a most remarkable event. There was a certain woman above four score

77

"The devilish bird flew high into the air, carrying with him the old witch from the bottom of the Vale'

years of age who had been imprisoned, indicted, and found guilty upon full evidence of that abominable sin of witchcraft, and for it was condemned to death.

'She gave out confidently that she was not going to die. However, on the appointed day she was taken from prison to the place of execution to be burnt alive.

'As she was escorted down the steps of La Tour Beauregard to

La Vallée de Misère, a great black raven hovered overhead, croaking in a most peculiar and doleful manner. As she was chained to the stake erected in her name she pleaded with a bystander to give her a clew of thread, which, having received, she fastened one end to her girdle and, with a mighty fling, threw the other end high up into the air towards the raven.

'The devilish bird stooped down and caught the thread with his beak, and flew high into the sky, carrying with him the old witch from the bottom of the Vale and up above the town's skyline. But wait! – A young man, alert to this desperate rescue bid, seeing her flying by, and being on top of the hill, flung his halberd so exactly between her and the raven that it sliced the thread asunder, and the old witch was caught again; but not before she had thrown many imprecations upon him and vomiting out whole cartloads of curses against him.

'However, she was taken back down to the stake and there, accordingly, burnt to ashes. But poor warder Gosselin – "ye holy wise providence of God so permitting it" – was in bitter short time brought on with an incurable disease, which he laid under with the most exquisite torments until, having languished some years, he was at last released from his sufferings by death.'

The account loses some of its effect when we find that no witches were sent to the stake in 1640.

Meanwhile, in Jersey, public executions were just as popular and a contemporary account by the diarist Jean Chevalier reveals that when Marie Esnouf was executed in 1648 the crowds were larger than when the Prince of Wales had visited, in 1646. Unlike poor Marie, of course, the Prince was allowed to leave the Island without having been strangled first.

In a way it shouldn't surprise us that these gruesome events were so popular. In the 16th and 17th centuries life was cheap, people were fascinated by the concept of death and suppressed by a dour, killjoy religion, so the chance of some sort of theatre, however macabre, had immediate appeal; the entertainment was also free.

The Islanders' deep-seated superstition allied to a deep mistrust of the French was also instrumental in ensuring that so many sorcerers to die.

Nearly a fifth of those people condemned as witches were French and although France might have had its fair share of alleged witches, at a time when the French were often at loggerheads with Great Britain, it was only natural that the Channel Islands occasionally felt threatened by unwanted visitors.

Another reason for this period of sustained witch-hunting has already been mentioned. There were people in the Channel Islands who genuinely believed that they had supernatural powers. They did go to a Friday night sabbat (the 'Gens Vendredi'), to a less formal 'ésbat' or to one of the most important meetings of the year, the 'Roodmas' of 30 April, where, drugged or affected by a self-induced hypnotic state, they were believed to dance back to back with other witches and, naked, copulated with all and sundry.

Ritual sacrifice would be made, the perverse 'osculum infamé' (the kiss of shame on the Devil's buttocks) would be given and eventually (so it was said), demons appeared in the midst of the assembly.

Before they left for home, tired devilmongers might be given powders or spells to use to foment more trouble in the parish; it was also said that some children had been born out of a chance encounter between their mother and the Devil at a sabbat (born from the 'jus primae noctis').

Be that as it may, in the 16th and 17th centuries not many witches seem to have benefited from their association with Satan and, as we shall see, by the time the 20th century came along the fortunes of some of their descendents hadn't improved much either.

Few of the sabbats on those bleak nights all those years ago had much to do with paganism; instead they were often Christian versions of what witches were believed to do. They were anti-Christ meetings rather than a tribute to older gods, often attended by people who had a grudge to bear against the church or their neighbours and believed that by turning to the Devil they would be able to gain revenge.

To that extent we can have little sympathy for them; if they chose to follow evil, rather than renounce it, they knew full well what the consequences might be.

Sympathy, though, can be extended to those people who were

caught up in the witch scare, and John Calvin can be blamed, to some extent, for his role in suggesting that superstitious people were often in league with the Devil. John Calvin, however, did not live in the Channel Islands – unlike a small group of people we have only mentioned in passing but whose influence and judgements can no longer be ignored.

Of the Crown officials who ruled the Islands during the most vigorous witch-hunts, the names of two families continually appear. Linked by marriage and by deeply-felt religious and political commitment, the de Carterets and Paulets between them condemned many of the sorcerers already named, doing so out of an unshakeable belief that the Devil was a regular visitor to these Channel Island shores.

CHAPTER 5

WITCH-FINDERS

THE de Carterets have been one of the most influential families in Channel Island history and they were at the peak of their power between the years 1550 and 1650.

Such was their influence in Jersey politics that, in 1642, enemies of Sir Philippe de Carteret, Lieutenant-Governor, Bailiff and Receiver-General, charged him with nepotism – with some justification. One of his cousins was Attorney-General, his brother was Solicitor-General, one of his nephews and three of his cousins were jurats, and of the 12 captains of the militia, seven were de Carterets, two more were nephews and one was a brother-in-law. It was a formidable line-up; all resulting from the marriage of Margaret Harliston to an earlier Philippe de Carteret, Lord of St Ouen's Manor, in the 15th century. She bore 20 sons and one daughter, and most of them eventually assumed their rightful place in Jersey society.

One of the sons, Helier de Carteret, did especially well. He became Bailiff and held that position at the same time as Sir Hugh Vaughan, lecher and land-grabber, was Governor.

The two men, with vastly different personalities, had more than one heated exchange. As Bailiff between 1521 and 1557, Helier encouraged Huguenot preaching and happily confiscated Catholic endowments on behalf of the Crown (until Queen Mary came to the throne). His daughter, Margaret, married his nephew (also called Helier de Carteret) and, as seigneur (lord) of St Ouen, the younger man became senior jurat and leader of what was known as the Puritan party. Under Queen Mary he refused to go to mass and was one of the Islanders who crossed to Normandy to receive Holy Communion in the Huguenot church in St Lo.

In 1556, worried about the future of Sark, especially after its recent use by French pirates who had been expelled in 1553, he persuaded Queen Elizabeth to allow him the Island on condition that he made an annual payment of 50 shillings to the Crown and kept 40 able-bodied men on the land at all times in case of invasion.

Amias Paulet, brother of George and father of Anthony. 'Both George and Anthony ruled the Island with even greater rigour than Amias ever practised, their behaviour sometimes amounting almost to tyranny'

Local men, plus a few English people living in Jersey, were sent from the largest Channel Island to one of the smallest islands to begin a new life there, accompanied by the Presbyterian minister Cosme Brévint, who had been hand-picked for the job by Helier de Carteret. He didn't know it at the time, but by appointing Brévint as a minister, Helier was ensuring that Sark remained a Presbyterian stronghold long after his death.

L A T E

Memorable Providences

Relating to

Witchcrafts and *Poſſeſſions,*

Clearly Manifeſting,

Not only that there are Witches, but
that Good Men (as well as others)
may poſſibly have their Lives ſhortned
by ſuch evil Inſtruments of Satan.

**Frontispiece of the second edition of Cotton Mather's book
printed in 1691 both in Boston and London. He was
prominent in the Salem Witch Trials, as was his father,
Increase, who for three years had been a
chaplain in Guernsey**

With Sark populated and made Presbyterian, the Seigneur of St
Ouen turned back to his affairs closer at home. He began the
painstaking task of rooting out evil, and particularly sorcery, where-
ever he saw it. It was easier to do this in his own parish, and it is
no coincidence that St Ouen eventually provided more witches for
trial before the Royal Court than any other parish. For the de
Carterets did not like either Popery or sorcery and often muttered
curses against both of them in the same breath.

Perhaps there was a more cynical reason for this hatred of St
Ouen witches for, as Seigneur, de Carteret could claim the property
of anyone condemned who had been living in his fief. This was a

very useful sideline to have when times were hard and, if he wanted, Helier could also request that a prisoner be executed on his own private gallows. This would have been scant comfort to Michelle la Blanche Vestue, who died on the gibbet of Hurés, St Ouen, in 1562.

While Helier and other members of the de Carteret family wielded a great deal of power in Jersey, another family, this time originating from Crewkerne in Somerset, was also starting to make a name for itself in local affairs. The Island connection began in 1549 when Sir Hugh Paulet (also spelt Poulet or Poulett) was appointed Governor of Jersey. Almost immediately, Sir Hugh and the elder Helier de Carteret, Bailiff, became friends. They had a lot in common, particularly their religious beliefs (Helier actually died in Sir Hugh's London house in 1561), although it would appear that Sir Hugh was not extreme in his views and was thus able to continue to prosper during Queen Mary's brief reign.

His two sons, Amias and George, on the other hand, who, from the middle of the 16th century to the beginning of the 17th were at various times Lieutenant-Governor, Governor, Bailiff, church elder or jurat, were much fiercer in their admiration for John Calvin.

Amias, for example (Lieutenant-Governor in 1556 and Governor when his father died in 1571) went on a happy-go-lucky rout of Catholicism after Queen Mary died.

He smashed all of the remaining statues of the saints at Mont Orgueil and ordered that altar slabs be turned into gun platforms. It was Amias who encouraged Guillaume Morise to set up the first Reformed Church in St Helier and he also persuaded Queen Elizabeth to allow the use of the Calvinistic Book of Divine Service in Jersey.

His son, Anthony, eventually succeeded as Governor in 1590. Like many of the de Carteret family, Amias perversely equated Catholicism with sorcery and hated both; but it was brother George who became the most successful witch-finder of Jersey. Born in 1534, George Paulet served as either Bailiff or Lieutenant-Governor for nearly 60 years before he died in the 17th century at the goodly age of 86.

He was an honourable man, and looked after his daughter's nine children when their father, Sir Philippe de Carteret, died in 1594. He was also one of the elders of the Town Church, a serving Commissioner to Guernsey (which he frequently visited) and, in 1583, when he was sworn in as Bailiff, his oath of office included the following: '(You) will defend the rights of the true Christian Church, and secure to the utmost of your power the destruction, annihilation, and abolition of the false Church of the Pope, and that all who despise the pure Word of God shall be condignly punished.'

George hated Catholicism and sorcery and was never afraid to come down heavily on the side of his version of the Christian law when supposedly evil people were brought before him.

As Bailiff, he sat in judgement on at least 35 suspected witches; of these, 18 were executed. He was married four time, his last wife taken in 1604 when he was 70. A young man at heart, he still managed to father two children before his death in 1621.

Meanwhile, Guernsey was also experiencing a sudden rush of witch-hunting which had a lot to do with the appointment of Amice de Carteret, second son of Helier (coloniser of Sark) and godson to Amias Paulet, who was created Bailiff in March, 1601. Amice was perceived as a good man.

Originally a jurat, Deputy-Bailiff and church elder in Jersey before being offered the post of Chief Magistrate in the other island, he was described as 'a man of great repute and much beloved by the people' in the 1585 'Chroniques of Jersey'. He was also a man with the common touch and, in 1594, had tried to improve the wage of eight pence per day that workmen at Elizabeth Castle were receiving.

Perhaps the common touch deserted Amice when he took up his new post in Guernsey for, in all, he was concerned with at least 65 witch trials between March 1601 and April 1631 (his predecessor had presided over two). Among the 65 'witches', 35 were burnt and 19 banished.

If he felt obliged to outdo George Paulet in Jersey in his pursuit of Devilry he undoubtedly succeeded, but he was true to his faith and made no bones about three pet hates – Romanism, Anglicanism and witchcraft. All three were abhorrent to him and the way that at least two of them were linked can, perhaps, be seen in the following

Court decree of 1611 which was initiated by the Bailiff: All Catholic idolators who persisted in their obstinate ignorance and showed that they had not renounced the abominations of Antichrist were to be hunted down and brought before the court to receive condign punishment.

WHEN King James I came to the English throne in 1603 and tried to instil Anglicanism in the Islands Amice de Carteret was one of its fiercest critics.

Born to Calvinism, de Carteret was determined to keep his people dependent on Presbyterian authority as long as possible, which is one of the main reasons why Guernsey only slowly turned towards the King's religion. For 19 years, until 1629, Amice was both Bailiff and Lieutenant-Governor, which meant that his power over people's lives was immense. Significantly, after his death on 19 April 1631, the number of Islanders accused of witchcraft and sent to the stake fell sharply, while it was in Jersey where the witch trials lingered longest, continuing until 1661 under the de Carteret régime.

Marie Le Dain, wife of Jean Le Dain, was the last person to be executed for sorcery in the Channel Islands. She was sentenced on 31 January 1660 after '24 good people' from her own parish and two of the parishes next to her own had decided that she was guilty.

That she was a housewife from St Ouen, and therefore a parishioner from de Carteret territory, seems quaintly appropriate. Michelle La Blanche Vestue, one of the first Jersey women to be executed for witchcraft 99 years before, had also been a housewife in this uncompromising parish.

POSTSCRIPT: BY the end of the 17th century the Channel Islands seemed to have come to their senses. In a more enlightened age, so-called witches were no longer being burnt at the stake. However this does not mean that parishioners had lost any of their superstitious belief, nor that they weren't afraid to take the law into their own hands.

The text shown on the next page, from a Trinity burial register, in Jersey, and written by the Rector about Elizabeth Gavey, shows

that there could be sympathy for 'the accused' and it would have
been written after Elizabeth had been given a decent Christian burial.

It translates as: 'Elizabeth Gavey was buried on the 29th day of
March, 1765. She was found dead on the morning of the 28th near
La Mare d'Angot at Ville a l'Evèque.

'Killed by miserable superstitious people accusing her of sorcery
who, after having cruelly mistreated her, caused her to die, throwing
there her poor body.

'She was a poor innocent, who was thus born and lived all her
life a poor innocent.'

There is no evidence of a trial but as we have seen before, with
the superstitious Rondel family in 1930 and as we will see again in
the 20th century in Guernsey, just because you no longer 'put
witches to the question' didn't mean that you no longer believed
that evil people, with unnatural powers, couldn't frighten you half
to death.

CHAPTER 6

THE OLD WORLD MEETS THE NEW

IN late 1692 Cotton Mather, one of the most influential Puritan ministers in Boston, New England, wrote in his book 'Wonders of the Invisible World': 'We have been advised by some Credible Christians yet alive that a Malefactor, accused of witchcraft as well as Murder, and Executed in this place more than Forty Years ago, did then give notice of a Horrible Plot against this Country by Witchcraft, and a foundation of Witchcraft then laid, which ... would probably Blow Up, and Pull Down, all the Churches in this Country. And we have now with Horror seen the discovery of such a Witchcraft!

'An Army of Devils is openly broke in upon the place which is the Centre ... and the houses of the Good People are fill'd with the doleful Shrieks of their Children and Servants, Tormented by Invisible Hands, with Tortures preternatural.'

Witchcraft had arrived in Salem.

YET the year 1692 had begun so differently. There was, admittedly, some superstition and harmless white magic in the village but nothing substantial until, towards the end of February, strange things began to happen in the household of the local minister, Samuel Parris. Parris's daughter, Elizabeth, aged about nine, and his 11-year-old niece, Abigail Williams, were seen creeping under chairs and stools and acting in a most peculiar fashion.

They uttered strange oaths and foolish words and sometimes threw themselves into convulsions during which they twisted their limbs in hideous fashion.

The minister's first attempts at a cure were by prayer, but this only had a temporary effect.

The girls, the minister discovered with alarm, had been dabbling in the occult. In attempting to see who their future husbands would be they had 'conjured up a spectre in the shape of a coffin'.

Within a few days the girls' odd behaviour had spread to several

Courtroom scene in Salem during the trials

of their friends. These included 12-year-old Ann Putnam (who eventually became a notorious 'devil-raiser'), Mary Warren, aged 20, Mercy Lewis, 19, Mary Walcott, 16, and Elizabeth Hubbard, aged 17. The fits, though, were generous in their movements and other women – including Ann Putnam's mother – and goodwives Pope, Bibber and Goodall, were all affected as the year continued.

Why these women were affected has never been satisfactorily explained, but Parris's initial concern was much simpler ... what was he to do with an assortment of young girls who were writhing on the floor, uttering strange and unhealthy noises?

In their more lucid moments Elizabeth Parris and Abigail Williams explained that Tituba, a Carib Indian slave, who worked in the Parris household, had shown them how to look into the future. They had done this in a way similar to that of divination via a crystal ball, but the white of an egg, poured into a glass, is looked at instead of a piece of crystal.

In a society dominated by Puritanism the whole matter smelt of

Devilry – at least it did so to minister Parris. But more names were needed, and once Tituba was imprisoned and questioned by the local magistrates, who were equally concerned by the strange behaviour of the Salem girls, Sarah Good and Sarah Osborne were indicted, arrested and charged with the crime of sorcery ... Tituba's testimony was to initiate the Salem witch-hunt.

In any other society much of what was to follow could have been avoided, but as well as being intensely Puritanical, Salem was unfortunate in its choice of church and political leaders: its magistrates weren't overly impressive, either.

One of them, John Hathorne, obviously enjoyed his role of witch-finder general and on the flimsiest of evidence was willing to accept that a suspect was involved with Satan. His questioning of suspects was also highly contentious and always implied guilt rather than innocence.

For example, similar questioning techniques to those used in Guernsey generations before were used when a suspect was arrested. Leading questions such as: 'When did you first make contact with the Devil?' were asked, which left the accused in the impossible position of having to defend himself or herself from a charge which had already been accepted as proven.

As well as magistrates like John Hathorne, Sarah Good had to contend with the testimonies of her husband and daughter. On oath William Good swore: 'He was afraid that she (his wife) either was a witch or would be one very quickly.' Not a very reassuring comment from your husband. He added that he had seen a strange 'tit' or 'wart' on his wife's body, implying that she was used to suckling one of the Devil's pets, or familiars.

Dorcas Good, Sarah's four-year-old daughter, was equally unimpressive as a character witness. She condemned her mother as a witch and added detail to her father's statement, saying that she had seen three familiars feeding from her devil-mother: '... three birds, one black, one yellow ... and that these birds hurt the children and afflicted persons.'

A different form of 'evidence' accepted and used against Sarah Good was revealed when the afflicted girls were taken to look at the accused woman.

When they stood close to her they immediately began to howl in terror and pain, calling out that Sarah's spectral presence was biting and pinching them, even when she was physically some yards away. Whenever the girls looked the other way the fits stopped. To an impressionable man like Hathorne, this was evidence enough of her guilt.

As Sarah Good became further immersed in her role of wicked witch, Sarah Osborne viewed the proceedings with growing horror – especially when Tituba was called to the witness box. The Carib slave, who eventually escaped punishment herself, admitted her involvement with the supernatural and then talked about seeing a thing 'with wings and two legs and a head like a woman' suckling from Mrs Osborne. She also accused her of having signed her name in the 'Devil's Book' and, when the afflicted girls were brought before Osborne, they threw themselves into a convulsive frenzy, just as they had done in front of Sarah Good.

By the middle of March, Martha Cory and Rebecca Nurse had been added to the list of suspects. Three of the afflicted girls in particular accused them, the three being Ann Putnam, Abigail Williams and Elizabeth Parris. The eldest of them was just 12 years old.

Martha and Rebecca were of good standing in the village. Rebecca, in particular, was a kindly and devout Christian, and her arrest shocked the local community so much that certain villagers presented a petition to the magistrates, on her behalf, asserting her innocence.

By now, though, the power that the supposedly afflicted girls were able to exert on the magistrates and the atmosphere in the courts were such that even neutral observers found it hard to make a reasoned judgement of what was happening. Whenever one of the accused so much as moved, or sighed, the girls would twist and turn in a most irreligious way. Even more alarming were alleged physical signs of spectral damage being done to the girls.

If, for example, Martha Cory bit her lips because she was nervous, at least one of the afflicted children would complain that she felt pain in her lips and, it was said, a bite mark would appear there, to prove that what she had said was true.

Without doubt the court records were supposed to be accurate when they explained that real physical damage occurred to an afflicted girl if a suspect injured herself in any way. It could have be auto-suggestion which caused this injury-transference but, no matter what the cause, it was another nail in the suspect's coffin.

Incredibly, Martha Cory was charged with the crime of 'biting her lip' and when she complained, quite rightly, that she saw no harm in it, the Reverend Nicholas Noyes of neighbouring Salem Town explained: 'I believe it is apparent she practiseth witchcraft in the congregation, there is no need of image.'

What Reverend Noyes was saying, in effect, was that instead of sticking pins into clay models of her accusers and hurting them that way, she was using her own body as an image of her assailants and so, by deliberately hurting herself, she was hurting them.

BY April the villagers were living in the midst of an evil that threatened everyone, and the time should have been ripe for one of the more respected members of the Salem community – perhaps a clergyman – to ease the tension with a few well-chosen words.

Those words were delivered on 3 April by the Reverend Samuel Parris. In front of a packed congregation he chose for his sermon lines from St John, Chapter VI. They included the following: *'Jesus answer them, have I not chosen you twelve, and one of you is a devil? He spake of Judas Iscariot the son of Simon: for he it was that should betray him, being one of the twelve.'*

(John Chapter 6: verses 70-71)

The inference the good minister was making was that Rebecca Nurse, like Judas before her, had betrayed Christ after being taken into His confidence. Parris believed that this rather deaf and mild-mannered woman had been won over by the Devil and he was prepared to condemn her, even before she had been put on trial.

Sarah Cloyse, Rebecca's sister, listened to this appalling sermon with disgust. Before it was through she had walked out and away from the minister's condemnation of her kith and kin, allowing the church door to slam behind her as she did so. The noise eventually became a kind of death knell, for within 24 hours she, too, was accused of sorcery.

**Execution – from the Witch Trials in Salem –
following condemnation and sentence**
(courtesy of the Salem Witch Museum)

After Parris's confident sermon against evil the number of people accused of witchcraft grew alarmingly. One of these, for the first time, was a man.

John Proctor and his wife, Elizabeth, were accused of being sorcerers when, ironically, they had been two of the community who had shown more than average normality in a world rapidly becoming dominated by spectres and demons.

Mary Warren, one of the afflicted girls, had been John Proctor's servant, and he had found a simple way of ridding her of the evil spirit that lurked within. As he explained to the court when he was placed on trial: ' ... when she was first taken with fits (I) kept her close to the wheel and threatened to thrash her, and then she had no more fits till the next day (when I) was gone, forsooth. And then she must have her fits again, forsooth.'

Obviously, whatever tormented her, Mary Warren was more

afraid of John Proctor than the Devil and, to her credit, Mary Warren recognised it. She tried to assert her master's innocence. Unfortunately, she could not do so with too much enthusiasm for if she did she would have been denounced as a witch herself. So, when Abigail Williams and Ann Putnam swore that they had seen farmer John Proctor and his wife sign the Devil's Book, Mary Warren reluctantly agreed that this was so.

Her testimony helped to destroy her master for, while Elizabeth Proctor was eventually released after pleading that she was large with child and therefore in no fit state to be hanged, for husband John there was no escape. He went to the gallows convicted of witchcraft on 19 August 1692.

WITHOUT doubt the most important person arrested during the Salem witch-trials was George (or Georgius) Burroughs, who was himself a church minister, albeit a rather lapsed one.

On 20 April Ann Putnam saw Burroughs in a vision, and this tenuous evidence led to his arrest, even though Ann had been only two years old when Burroughs had been a preacher in Salem, in 1680. The vision reappeared and with it came the spectres of Burrough's first two wives, who had both died while still married to their husband. The spectres, according to Ann, accused Burroughs of murdering them. The minister was duly summoned to the court from nearby Wells, where he was working.

He appeared in front of the magistrates on 4 May.

By now some of the other girls were seeing Burroughs in their visions. They cringed in terror when he looked at them and Hathorne had no doubt that this was one of the main leaders in Salem's witching community. Apart from the girls' testimony, Burroughs had begun to condemn himself from his own mouth, confessing that his house was 'haunted with toads'.

He also admitted that only one of his children had been confirmed. Even more damning to the jury and to the magistrates was evidence of Burrough's violent temper and great strength, which had occasionally scared his first two wives. So the rough-necked minister joined an ever-growing number of other men and women in jail, all wondering what their eventual fate would be.

The Governor of Massachusetts (the state in which Salem lay) at that time was Sir William Phips, an ardent Puritan and a protégé of Cotton Mather and his father, Increase. Both members of the Mather family were powerful ministers in the state and, on Increase's advice, the Governor ordered a Commission to be set up to examine all of the evidence and to bring those who had been accused of witchcraft to trial.

On 27 May a special court of Oyer and Terminer was convened under acting chief-justice William Stoughton, but the mood of the Inquiry had already been established. Governor Phips, afraid that all of the sorcerers who were currently in prison would practise devilish spells, ordered them to be placed in irons. Obviously he believed that witchcraft was alive and well and living in Salem. From the witches' point of view, more bad news was swift to follow – John Hathorne, the magistrate and witch-finder, was included on the Commission.

By this time the Salem witch-hunt had claimed its first victim. On 10 May, Sarah Osbourne, one of the first women to be accused of witchcraft, died in jail. Exactly a month later the next victim was to die.

On 10 June, after a series of witnesses had spoken against her and after dolls with pins stuck through them had been found in her house, Bridget Bishop was condemned as a witch and led to the gallows. She was certainly a cantankerous old woman but, apart from the discovery of the dolls, her worse crime had been to allow people into her home late at night to drink and to play shovel-board. In a society rigorously entrenched in Puritanism, such behaviour was scandalous.

Bridget Bishop might have led less than a blameless life but at least one of the next five victims sentenced by the court of Oyer and Terminer was the most timid of creatures. When Rebecca Nurse, who had been languishing in jail for well over a month before being brought before the court was eventually tried, she was rightly found not guilty.

Even John Hathorne seemed satisfied by this decision; but it did not satisfy the afflicted girls who had brought the charge against her in the first place. Among others, Ann Putnam's mother testified that Rebecca Nurse's spectre had tried to choke her to death, and Abigail Hobbes and her mother, Deliverance (both notoriously unreliable witnesses), spoke loudly against this unfortunate woman. Without the storm that these women created, chief-justice Stoughton would almost certainly have accepted the not guilty verdict but, ignoring his role as impartial arbiter, he expressed his disapproval of the jury's decision and asked them to reconsider.

Rebecca Nurse was questioned again. Confused and rather deaf, she remained silent when asked about her association with other witches. Because of this silence a rather shame-faced jury found her guilty at the second time of asking and she was sentenced to die along with Sarah Good, Susannah Martin, Elizabeth Howe and Sarah Wildes.

Even a lengthy petition, presented to Governor Phips pleading her innocence, failed to save her from execution and on 19 July she was hanged. She would have been as bewildered in her death as she was humble in her life – but not so Sarah Good. Defiant to the end she refused to admit her guilt and, when asked by the Reverend Nicholas Noyes to confess her association with the Devil, on her way to being hanged, she retorted: 'You are a liar! ... I am no more a witch than you are a wizard and if you take away my life, God will give you blood to drink!' which, according to legend, was a prophetic statement, for when the Reverend Noyes lay dying some 25 years later, blood flowed copiously from his mouth.

So, the floodgates had been well and truly opened and, with six suspects already hanged, there were many more just waiting to follow.

ON 5 August six more suspects were brought to trial, including John and Elizabeth Proctor, John Willard, Martha Carrier of nearby Andover, George Jacobs and the Reverend George Burroughs. Jacobs and Burroughs had already been searched for witchmarks and, although none had been found on Burroughs, three 'tetts' had been discovered on Jacobs.

When a pin was run through two of them, Jacobs felt no pain – surely he suckled the Devil. So, with evidence like this, it was clear that he had little chance of reprieve. Yet it was really Burroughs who the afflicted girls were eager to punish, though for what real reason is unclear.

Young Ann Putnam virtually destroyed him completely, for part of her testimony reads as follows: 'Then immediately appeared to me the form of two women in winding-sheets, and napkins above their heads, at which I was greatly affrighted. And they turned their faces towards Mr Burroughs and looked very red and angry and told him that he had been a cruel man to them, and that their blood did cry for vengeance against him, and also told him that they should be clothed with white robes in Heaven when he should be cast into Hell. And immediately he vanished away.

'And as soon as he was gone the two women turned their faces towards me and looked as pale as a white wall, and told me that they were Mr Burrough's two first wives and that he had murdered them. And one told me that she was his first wife, and he stabbed her under the left arm and put a piece of sealing-wax on the wound. And she pulled aside the winding-sheet and showed me the place, and also told me that she was in the house (where) Mr Parris now lived where it was done ...

'And the other told me that Mr Burroughs and that wife which he hath now killed her in the vessel as she was coming to see her friends, because they would have one another.'

The girls had their way. Burroughs, as well as Willard, Jacobs, John Proctor and Martha Carrier were executed on 19 August. Ironically, 11 years later, in 1703, they were all officially pardoned – scarce recompense for Proctor's widow and her young child.

Meanwhile, 19 August 1692, did not pass without incident.

First was the dignified way that George Burroughs accepted his fate. On the ladder leading to the gallows he made a speech of such 'solemn and serious expressions as were to the admiration of all present', according to one of the bystanders.

When he finished this he recited the Lord's Prayer so fervently that it seemed that the watching crowd might cut him down and set him free. This did not please Mr Cotton Mather, who had been watching the proceedings with interest.

Realising that Burrough's declaration of innocence was turning the mob against the execution and that the former minister might

Increase Mather who, between April 1659 and March 1661, was chaplain of Castle Cornet in Guernsey

still gain his freedom, Mather made his own speech, declaring that the convicted man was no ordained minister and that the Devil had the ability to change his shape and voice at will: by doing so Satan could beguile the most scrupulous of people.

Burroughs was hanged.

In the 'Wonders of the Invisible World', written after this gristly pantomime, Cotton Mather spent a good deal of time justifying what he had done. He truly believed that poor George Burroughs was evil, saying that, at some time, he had been 'head actor of the hellish rendezvous' of at least eight self-confessed witches. He also believed that no man could lift a full barrel of molasses as Burroughs had done: only the Devil could make a man so strong.

A second macabre touch to the execution came after the hanging, when the corpses had been cut down to be buried. Burroughs, Willard's and Martha Carrier's bodies were all placed in the same shallow grave, in such a way that Burrough's chin and a hand and a foot of one of the others, remained uncovered. No-one in Salem was prepared to cover them up because to do so would, inevitably, lead to another arrest – why should a Christian help one of Satan's followers unless he himself had connections with the Devil?

On 22 September eight more victims were hanged. Sixteen in all had been condemned, but five changed their plea to guilty and were reprieved (the court felt it was not too late for them to plead with God for forgiveness). And one escaped, one pleaded she was with child, and Margaret Jacob was sent back to jail because she had an 'imposthume' (an abscess) on her head. The magistrates decided that she ought to get better before she died.

Meanwhile poor Giles Cory, an elderly farmer, refused to make any plea when he was questioned. This obstinacy in refusing to plead either guilty or not guilty so upset the court of Oyer and Ter-miner that he was held to be 'mute of malice', an offence punish-able by a fate worse than any of those so far mentioned.

Giles Cory was the first person in New England to be literally pressed to death. He was made to lie down before heavy weights were placed on his chest and then for two, agonising days, any breath he had was squeezed out of his body. Even when his tongue had to be forced back into his mouth by the Sheriff's cane, as the pain became so terrible, even then he refused to acknowledge the court's demands.

A contemporary wrote in his diary for 19 September 1692: *'About noon, at Salem, Giles Cory was pressed to death for stand-ing mute. Much pains were used with him (for) two days, one after another, by the court and Captain Gardner of Nantucket who had been of his acquaintance, but all in vain.'*

Samuel Sewall's Diary, 1692

It was all very unpleasant and begs the question – why did Cory choose such a wretched end? Well, he died silently to prevent his property from being confiscated by the court. If he had pleaded guilty or not guilty the court had the right to claim his possessions for the King so, by accepting *peine forte et dure*, he was denying officialdom this right of seizure. Giles Cory was not always pleasant to his family, but he owned valuable farmland which he wanted to go to his children. Hence his prolonged ordeal.

By this time 21 people had died, another eight had been condemned and were waiting to be hanged, and 250 suspects had been called to trial. The Devil seemed to be everywhere – but what connection is there between his presence in New England and the history of witchcraft in the Channel Islands?

'TO discover the trade of your husband-to-be, throw the white of a raw egg into a glass of water and expose it to the rays of the noonday sun, in preference at Christmas or Midsummer. The egg, in coagulating, assumes curious and fantastic forms, and any young girl brave enough to look into the egg looks into the future. If not his name, the girl who tries this charm will see the trade or profession of the man whom she will marry.'

Old Guernsey superstition

ON 25 February 1692, when most good people in Salem were busily at work, unaware that Satan was in their midst, Mary Sibley was persuading the Carib Indian slaves John and Tituba to prepare witch-cake, so that the community's afflicted children might be cured.

They did so, and a mixture of meal and the children's urine was placed in a tin and baked in the fire. The 'cake' that was made was then fed to the Parris family's pet dog, presumably in the hope that any spirits tormenting the girls would be transferred to the animal. When news of this unappetising meal, given to his dog, reached the Reverend Samuel Parris, he was furious and described the act as 'going to the Devil for help against the Devil' ... but it was too late. The cake had been cooked and eaten and consequently Parris was more than ever convinced that Satanism had arrived in New England. He fumed that '(the Devil's) rage is vehement and terrible: and when he shall be silenced, the Lord only knows' ... but one fascinating aspect of this Satanic meal, which bears directly on this study is this: where had the recipe come from in the first place?'

More than likely it had been handed down to Tituba from an older member of the family or, perhaps, she had been told about witch-cakes from someone who had glanced at an earlier European grimoire.

After so many years, who can say? But it is interesting to note that the self-same recipe would probably have been known by a Tourgis or a Becquet in Guernsey some 60 years before. They would also have known how to use the white of an egg to look into the future, and egg-divination, as we know from earlier in this chapter, had led to the girls' 'affliction' in the first place. This is not meant to suggest that Tituba had any connection with the Channel Islands, but there are similarities between the two small Puritanical communities.

The Devil did not travel directly from the Channel Islands to New England to cause mischief there, but when the roots of the Salem witch-hunts are pulled up and examined, clinging to them tightly are several clumps of Channel Island earth.

TRADITIONALLY, the Channel Islands have produced excellent seamen, and the more adventurous of these have explored the world. So when America was looking for immigrants (and for ships to carry them), Guernsey and Jersey names appear in many contemporary documents. We know, for example, that in 1631 the merchant ship called 'Hope' was part-owned by John Bailache the Elder 'of the isle of Jersey, marchaunte', and that it made more than one trip to New England.

As well as providing Constables for the parish of St Lawrence, in Jersey, the Bailache family provided men who regularly plied a triangular shipping route between Europe, the West Indies, and New England. More than one member of the family settled in what is now Massachusetts and Bellyhak Hill in Salem was given that name by two of John Bailache's business partners. Meanwhile, in 1650 Charles I gave his loyal Governor of Jersey, George Carteret, a group of islands off the coast of Virginia known as Smith's Isles. At the time he was in no position to guarantee this gift because of his quarrel with Parliament, but in 1660 the monarchy was restored and Charles II was invited to be King.

He was more than grateful for the help that Carteret had given to his father. A sixth part of the Bahamas, an eighth part of Carolina and an area to the west of the Hudson, now to be called New Jersey, was ceded to the Governor. He was also invited to become a founder member of the Hudson Bay Trading Company.

With so much territory to control, Sir George Carteret needed governors to ensure that it remained his. He chose as first governor of New Jersey a young relative, Philippe de Carteret, who set sail for America in April, 1665.

The first settlement he created was Elizabethtown (named after his patron's wife). Initially it was a mere collection of four log cabins but a steady stream of other settlers arrived, many of them Channel Islanders, coming to New Jersey because old Jersey persisted in using the colony as a dumping ground for its unwanted paupers. Even so, the colony prospered and the population increased a great deal when, in 1674, a group of Quakers arrived from England.

For six years Quakers and Channel Islanders lived in harmony, but it was not to last. After Sir George Carteret's death in 1680 Sir Edmund Andros, governor of New York and seigneur of Sausmarez, Guernsey, decided that inter-island rivalry should continue in America and he began a political battle to destroy Philippe de Carteret's control of New Jersey, which was resolved (in Andros' favour) only after de Carteret had been viciously set upon by hired thugs in Andros' pay.

As the position for Channel Islanders in New Jersey worsened, a new wave of settlers had been making their homes in New England, away from the 'new' rather than 'old' Jersey, many of them brought to America by another member of the de Carteret family.

Philip English (originally L'Anglois), born in Trinity, Jersey, and grandson of the seigneur of St Ouen, had, by 1692, established a thriving shipping industry along the eastern American seaboard. He had also built for himself a fine house in Salem, staffed by as many as 15 Jerseymen and women. As we will see, by 1692 he was also trapped in the Salem witch-hunts.

But both before and after this fateful year other Channel Islanders arrived, including John Syvret, who was baptised at St Ouen in

April, 1644, and who died in Wenham, New England, in 1742 in his 98th year.

Other traditional Channel Island names that belonged to families who made their way across the Atlantic include Janvrin, Cabot, Le Marquand, Dumaresq, Messervy, Vaudin, Valpy, Touzel, Le Cornu and Poingdestre. Of these the Cabot family proved most influential.

For from the late 17th century onwards, John Cabot, born in 1680, and his son, Joseph, born in 1720 in Salem, eventually became two of the most influential immigrants to America through their dealings in the opium, rum and slave trades. Their lives and those of their burgeoning family deserve a book of their own (the Cabots were instrumental in building Harvard University), while, as we will see, another member of their family, many generations later, was to prove herself as adroit a woman (or witch) as you might ever see.

So it is that, according to Marion G. Turk in 'The Quiet Adventurers in North America' (Detroit, 1983) as many as 300 Channel Island names can be found in Massachusetts, with many of these being traced back to 17th century Salem.

So, when the magistrates were searching for witches in May 1692, they were doing so in a community where there were people who would have been told about Satan and his ways from parents and grandparents who knew the Devil when he was thought to be active in the Channel Islands.

One or two New Englanders with Channel Islands ancestry would also have known about witch-cakes – just one connection between the Old World and the New. And, if the Devil had visited Guernsey and Jersey, why shouldn't he also visit America?

Even the way of life in Salem had similarities with the Islands of some 60 or 70 years before. The community was close, superstitious and prepared to turn in upon itself to a frightening extent when it thought that it was being threatened. People were prepared to accept the most outrageous demands from their leaders, who were pious, Puritan and, at times, priggish. Some also had the mean streak which showed through when Cotton Mather intervened to make certain that George Burroughs died.

To his credit, Mather genuinely believed that the Devil was friendly with the condemned man but imagine the chaos he could have caused if he had been allowed to deal with Channel Island witches ... which brings us closer to home for, funnily enough, Mather could so easily have become a Guernseyman.

'MEN may NOT worship or PRAY unto Angels, Saints, or Graven images ... Alas! God has shut their eyes and given them up to a blind mind! And when it is thus with men, MIRACLES CANNOT convert them ... Should God open the bars of the bottomless PIT and let loose DEVILS and DAMNED WIGHTS to come flying and crying into our assemblies, with the CHAINS of DARKNESS rattling about them, to WARN sinners of the WRATH TO COME, and tell them what a dreadful place Hell is, neither would that comfort them.'

The author of this attack on sinful humanity was born in Massachusetts in 1637. He was called Increase because his father, Pastor Richard Mather, told his wife on hearing that she was pregnant for a sixth time: 'I have planted, but God gave the increase'. Surprisingly, between April 1659 and March 1661, young Increase was chaplain of Castle Cornet in Guernsey.

If he had been born a generation or so earlier he might have stayed, but Amice de Carteret had been dead for nearly 20 years and Increase disliked the Island's relaxed attitude towards religion, its allegiance to the King, and his immediate Christian superiors.

If he had stayed, and risen to any position of authority, who knows how many more witch trials he and his son, Cotton, would have perpetuated in Guernsey? But he returned instead to America, where the Mathers became so powerful that they could select and depose state governors.

In hindsight, Increase's decision to leave the Channel Islands was probably good news for any 'witches' still living there, but it was bad news for the wife of a Jerseyman living in Salem. Ann Pudeator (Poingdestre), whose husband probably knew all about witch trials and (before she was arrested) could have told her how they used to operate in the old country, was charged with sorcery midway through 1692.

Eventually, Ann was found guilty and hanged but the sentence was incredibly harsh, even for those times, for the evidence against her was provided by several of the hysterical afflicted girls who were used to seeing the Devil in anyone brought before them.

Her main 'crime', according to contemporary records was that of threatening the girls with her spectral being: one such young girl being Ann Putnam, who told the court that she had seen Mrs Pudeator flying through the air on a broomstick.

Sarah Churchill and Mary Warren also had their say and told the court that Pudeator had asked them to sign the 'Devil's Book' and to give their souls to Satan. They had refused, they said, and were consequently mocked and tormented by the woman.

By now the afflicted girls were living in a world so bizarre that they could not tell the difference between nightmare and reality. But the magistrates continued to listen to them and Ann was condemned to be taken from the court and hanged. She could easily have gone to the gallows full of hate: instead she asked for a little mercy and was even able to wish the magistrates well. 'I would humbly begg of yo'r honours to Take it into your Judicious and Pious consideration That my life may not be taken away by such false Evidence and witnesses as ... given in against me by Sarah Church and Mary Warren. I am altogether ignorant of and know nothing in the least measure about it nor nothing else concerning the crime of witchcraft for which I am condemned to die as will be known to men and angells att the great day of Judgment begging and imploring your prayers att the throne of grace in my behalfe and your poor and humble petition'r shall for ever pray as she is bound in duty for your hon'rs health and happiness in this life and eternall felicity in the world to come.'

Ann's humble petition fell on deaf ears. Because of the testimony of hysterical young girls, she was executed.

WHEN Jerseyman Philip English was caught up in the witch-hunts he not only survived them but returned to Salem where he was not as generous to his persecutors as Ann Pudeator had been, and it is easy to see why. For he was a rich man and, although he had escaped the gallows, he had lost part of his fortune and was to lose his wife.

As a Channel Islander in New England he had done well. He married into money and then used his wealth to build a fleet of ships which regularly took cod, rum, molasses and whale products to Europe; in return wine, brandy, Island knitwear and, shockingly, children were brought back to an appreciative American Market.

The children English imported to the New World were young boys and girls who were 'bought' from their parents in the Islands for about seven pence each. After purchase, they were yours to do with as you wished for a limited period, depending on to contract you had signed.

As Marion G. Turk explains: 'He (English) is probably one good reason for the presence in Mass. of so many Jersey persons and families, as he went into a side business of bringing into the colonies hundreds of Jersey and Guernsey boys and girls indentured to him, and bound out to others for servants, clerks, seamen and household help.'

Such indentures were not uncommon and English continued his people trade well into the 18th century.

So, by the time a warrant was made out for his arrest on 30 April 1692, he owned 21 ships, 14 buildings in Salem and was the town's well-respected benefactor, although wealth alone could not save him from persecution. On 31 May he was presented before the Court of Oyer and Terminer and charged as follows: 'In the Yeare aforesaid and divers other days and times as well as before and after Certain detestable Arts called Witchcraft and Sorceries, Wickedly Mallitiously and felloniously hath he used, Practised and Exercised At and in the Towne of Salem.'

Witnesses were summoned and English and his wife were imprisoned, but wealth and influence are an advantage and, with the aid of the Reverend Joshua Moody, the couple escaped from jail and fled to New York, where they were able to watch the final stages of the witch trials in comparative safety.

BY now the witch-hunt had assumed ridiculous proportions. Some of the afflicted girls were being taken out to other towns, like blood-hounds, to sniff out any sorcerers who might be lurking there. They were also finding animal-witches as well. More than one dog was put to death because it appeared in the hallucinations of one of the afflicted girls.

The situation was intolerable and peoplesuch as Joseph Dudley, the Chief Justice of New York, were no longer prepared to stand back and watch what was happening without attempting to halt the madcap course of events. Pressure was placed on Governor Phips to review the purpose of the original Commission and, despite strenuous objections from some of the presiding magistrates, on 28 October the special court of Oyer and Terminer was officially ended.

Consequences of that terrible year could not, and did not, begin and end with the setting up and closing down of such a destructive piece of legal machinery. The effects of decisions taken by the court lingered on for generations, and even now no-one is quite sure if there really was just a little bit of Satanism in Salem or whether the whole ugly affair had been the result of an over-keen puritan administration. In 1693 all of those still implicated for the crime of witchcraft were officially pardoned. In December, 1696, Judge Samuel Sewall, one of the original prosecuting magistrates, publicly asked the Salem community for forgiveness ... which is something neither Increase or Cotton Mather ever did.

Eventually, the Reverend Samuel Parris, who had done so much to inflame a situation which was bad enough already, and a man who had hounded Rebecca Nurse and others to their deaths, was forced to leave town. His congregation was no longer prepared to put up with such a sanctimonious humbug.

Even young Ann Putnam tried to redress the balance in 1706 by publicly asking God and her fellow Christians to forgive her sins.

AND afterwards, after the events of 1692?

Well, some sort of sanity returned to Salem, and while the authorities eventually gave financial compensation to the relatives of those they had executed, and George Burroughs was even read-mitted to the church, no-one could undo death.

Philip English realised this more than most. His wife was to die in 1694 and he was certain that her early demise had been brought on by the six weeks she had spent in prison. He had also lost a good deal of his property when he was arrested, some of it seized by the mob. Meanwhile he was languishing in jail, £1,500 worth was taken by the local Sheriff, George Corwin.

Although Corwin had taken this on behalf of the Crown and most of it was eventually returned, a Channel Islander never forgets and in 1697 the redoubtable grandson of the seigneur of St Ouen is al-leged to have chosen a particularly macabre form of revenge.

Before his death Sheriff Corwin had owed a lot of money. So as soon as he had left the land of the living English bought a suit for debt against his estate and then made it clear that he would seize Corwin's body in settlement if it were removed from the premises where it lay. The relatives of the dead man had to scurry around for enough money to buy back Corwin's property while the corpse lay rotting in their midst: it was quite a time before the debt was finally settled and the corpse removed.

BEFORE leaving Salem and the events of 1692 it is worth looking back at some of the more fascinating aspects of that year.

Undoubtedly the village created around itself an atmosphere similar to one which Channel Islanders had known in earlier years. There were the same fears about neighbours; the worry in case you were the next one to be taken away; the same inflexible hierarchy, which it was almost impossible to placate, with magistrates and preachers more interested in proving guilt than innocence.

Yet there were pronounced differences between Salem and Guernsey or Jersey of 60 years before. The courtroom in the New England village was dominated by passion, and by howling girls who writhed in terror as people were brought before them. No spec-tral evidence condemned a man or women in the Channel Islands whereas in Salem it did. And in Salem where were the sabbats, the orgies that witches are supposed to attend? Presumably, copulating with the Devil wasn't popular in New England in 1692.

It also seems ironic that suspects who admitted that they were witches were never executed. Only those who denied their guilt went to the gallows, because it was felt that while a self-confessed witch could always spend her life repenting, a convicted witch was an obvious threat to the community. Refusing to admit guilt deserved death, and the effect of this strange logic can be imagined. Terrified prisoners gladly confessed that they practised sorcery if it kept them alive, and they were quite prepared to denounce neighbours and friends if it diverted attention away from them, and pleased the magistrates.

On the other hand, if anyone showed outright contempt for the leaders of the community who were perpetrating the witch hunts, or deemed that witchcraft was a threat to the community, then he (or she) was dicing with death.

But now we come to a final curious Channel Island connection in our American story.

THREE hundred and fifty years after the last Salem 'witch' had been pardoned, Laurie Cabot moved to the town from nearby Lexington. She was in her early thirties and a descendant of Jerseyman John Cabot, who on 14 June 1700 and along with his brother, George, gave power of attorney to his mother, Suzanne (Gruchy) Cabot, and to Charles Marett, for the sale of his property in the Island before emigrating to New England with another brother, Francis.

Laurie Cabot is a unique figure in recent New England folklore and, at the time of writing, you can look her up on the internet, where she invites you to join her 'every Thursday evening at 10 pm to psychically travel 700 feet straight up over Salem, (where) you will see a crystal wheel surrounding the entire perimeter of the city of Salem.' This crystal wheel was placed there in 1975 by the Black Doves of the Isis Coven of the Cabot Tradition. You may go there to seek solace and help or you may go there to offer solace and help to others from all over the world.

Photographer Gary Grimshaw's picture of the 'official' witch of Salem, descended from the Cabots of Jersey, Laurie Cabot

Laurie Cabot had only been in Salem a short while before her pet cat was caught at the top of a tree. Despite frantic phone calls no-one, including the fire service and the police, would fetch it down, claiming: 'She'll come down when she's hungry. You'll never see cat bones hanging in a tree.' They weren't interested. So Laurie decided enough was enough, maintaining that her cat was her familiar and that she wanted action taken immediately.

Within an hour the authorities were knocking at her door, keen to set the animal free. No-one, it appeared, wanted Laurie to cast a spell on them. Since that day, in the early 1960s, Laurie Cabot, who was born Mercedes Elizabeth Kearsey in 1933 in Wewoka, Oklahoma, and who grew up in California before going to New England, has made a name for herself as one of the most prominent witches in the world. Married twice and now quite elderly, she is a descendant of the Jersey Cabots (her two children were christened Jody and Penny Cabot). The Boston Cabot family is hugely influential in America, to such an extent that one direct descendant is currently one of president Barack Obama's chief advisers.

Meanwhile, while taking pride in her Cabot ancestry, Laurie 'feels an affinity with a mysterious witch from (my) ancient Jersey lineage, who lived some 4,000 or 5,000 years ago.'

The former owner of 'The Cat, The Crow and the Crown' on Pickering Wharf ('The Official Witch Shoppe'), she asserts that Wicca is 'traditionally and primarily a duotheistic religion centred upon the idea of gender polarity and the worship of a Moon Goddess and a Horned God'. Be that as it may, there is no doubt that Laurie Cabot's influence in New England has been huge. At the time of writing, for example, 13,371 'fans' have visited her website, where she insists that her Cabot Hermetic Temple is used only to produce good results, not bad.

She even has permission to perform wedding ceremonies. Hers is such a different world from that of the 17th century, when she would have run the risk of being put to the test ... and then being hanged along with other Salem 'witches', most of whom pleaded their innocence – and quite rightly so, because they *were* innocent.

'The punishment of witches' in a work commonly referred to as ' Laienspiegel'. First published in Mainz in 1509, it has been described as a 'layman's guide' to their punishment. The work was an important one, with 14 editions being produced in the 16th century

CHAPTER 7

THE WITCH TRIALS END

FOR over a hundred years witch trials were commonplace in the Channel Islands.

Islanders were taught that the Devil regularly walked down lonely country lanes, looking for lost souls, and although we might query his decision to come here when there was so much more of the world to choose from, there was a widely-held belief that he existed, in human form – a belief which ultimately led to many, many deaths.

Presbyterian Calvinism was mainly to blame; and if the witch trials were to be curbed this unflinching, diehard brand of Christianity needed to be curbed, too. It was firmly entrenched in the States Assembly, in the judiciary and in every parish until well into the 17th century, after which it met with strong resistance from the British government.

Initially, the Islands fought off this British challenge with mixed results. When James I came to the throne in 1603 and tried to convert the Guernsiaise to Anglicanism, his attempts were brushed aside by the Bailiff and by the persuasive tongue of John de la Marche, who represented the Island's colloque and insisted that all religious affairs should be left in the hands of the Islanders themselves. A disappointed James I backed down; he needed his subjects' loyalty more than he needed their religious acquiescence.

Meanwhile in Jersey, when Sir John Peyton was appointed Governor in 1603, he determined to rid the Island of any Calvin-inspired nonsense and, to a large extent he succeeded, despite a formidable amount of opposition.

Peyton was a staunch Church of England man as well as being a shrewd politician, and he managed to drive a wedge between the clergy and the leading laymen. He also had on his side a growing number of Islanders who were dissatisfied with their puritanical lives, not all of them evil-livers, but men and women of good character who disliked the inquisitorial proceedings of church authorities and the way that ministers and church elders saw themselves as civil as well as Christian mentors.

So, by careful manipulation and an iron resolve not to give in to any Presbyterian demands, almost single-handedly Peyton restored control of all ecclesiastical affairs to the Bishop of Winchester and his Island representative, Dean David Bandinel.

In 1623 when the King made it compulsory for all Jersey people to use the Anglican Book of Common Prayer in their churches (one of 58 canon laws agreed in that year) it was also stipulated that 'whoever shall impugn the government of the Church by Archbishops, Bishops and Deans, shall "ipso facto" be excommunicate'.

With these 58 laws in force (and they were to bind Jersey to England for the next 300 years) the political and religious influence of Presbyterianism was being eaten away, wholesale. Even so, it was a lingering, painful death, and Bailiffs and jurats with Presbyterian sympathies continued to be elected to office on many occasions after Peyton's death, in 1630.

While Jersey was being made to toe an Anglican line Guernsey continued to tread its own path. When the Civil War between King and Parliament reached the Channel Islands in 1651, the Island authorities were quick to give their support to Parliament in an attempt to avoid the King's religion.

For nine years this policy worked, but when Charles II was invited to the throne in 1660, the heady days of self-rule in religious matters were numbered. Although it needed British troops to help establish Anglicanism (in 1663 troops were sent to Guernsey to make certain that the new Dean, John de Sausmarez, was accepted by the community), eventually it stuck fast and, on the surface at least, Guernsey people had to accept that the old days had gone. Anglicanism wouldn't go away and fighting against it and its mainland authority was futile.

If Jersey and Guernsey continued to look for loopholes to prevent any change in their spiritual way of life, Alderney accepted its fate more equably and, in 1662, the Reverend Elie Picot began the transition towards the English Church without too much fuss.

He was a popular churchman and, by his death in 1696, Islanders had come to accept that all serious religious decisions would ultimately be taken in Winchester. Sark, on the other hand, remained defiantly Presbyterian until the end. The influence of the Brévint family was so well established that only after Elie Brévint's death in 1674 was Anglicanism, in the shape of priest Moise Benest, introduced into the Island.

BY 1674 all of the Channel Islands were ostensibly Anglican and Calvin's influence had become a thing of the past.

It had been 13 years since the last witch had been put on trial and even if Presbyterian had been stronger (and some Jersey parishes still talked of 'les presbytèries' right up until the 19th century) it is doubtful whether many more witches would have been executed between 1674 and the present time.

One of the main reasons for this was a change in attitude by Islanders who had reaped the benefit of the Presbyterian doctrine that everyone had a right to be educated. Sponsored by the same church which taught that witches lived and needed to be destroyed, schools had been built in nearly all of the parishes, so that as succeeding generations learnt more about their world, they began to realise that ignorance was an enemy and that superstition ws absurd. The rest of Europe was coming to a similar conclusion. In areas where witches weren't persecuted there had been no increase in the number of Satanic crimes, and the Devil hadn't appeared there more frequently for Friday night gatherings. Judges, too, (with a few exceptions) became keener on real, rather than hearsay evidence, and were bolder in standing firm against mobs who enjoyed a witch trial, to be followed by a good hanging and burning.

The last English judicial execution for witchcraft was in 1712 and, in the same year, there was a last attempt by the Church authorities to manipulate the law courts and force them into punishing sorcery by death. In that year, in Walkern, Hertfordshire, Jane Wenham was persecuted for conversing with the Devil in the form of a cat. Three clergymen testified against her and she was condemned to death.

The judge, however, obtained her pardon, much to the annoyance of both the clergy and the mob. The verdict stood but Jane lived. In 1736 the English laws against witchcraft were repealed.

In the same year Marie Godfray, wife of Etienne Machon, of St Saviour, was brought before Jersey's Ecclesiastical Court.

It is one of the last recorded instances of a woman being tried for the crime of sorcery in the Channel Islands and the details of the trial and subsequent punishment reveal a spirit of enlightenment which previous church authorities would have condemned. The Minute Book for 4 October 1736, reads: 'Marie Godfray, wife of Etienne Machon of St Saviour, for dabbling in the Forbidden Arts and unveiling things that are hidden.

'The said Godfray has promised to abstain from such practices in future, and moreover to disclose the names of any who approach her for this purpose. Neighbouring parishes are to be informed of this by the reading of this Act of the Court after the Nicene creed.' Marie had been lucky; if she had been brought before the court only a few years before she would almost certainly have been executed.

So, with the courts deciding that 'witchcraft' didn't, after all, dwell within the Islands and with the laws having been changed, was this evidence that no-one practised the 'Black Arts' any more?

In theory, by the mid-1750s, all of this superstitious nonsense leading to witch trials should have ended for good but we know this is not the case because of the death of poor Elizabeth Gavey in Trinity, in 1765, hounded by the mob.

Following that, a casual glance through the Gazette de Jersey of Saturday, 10 March, 1787, reveals the following: 'A worthy householder in St Brelade dreamt that a certain wizard appeared to him and ordered him to poison himself at a date to be specified. He was enjoined not to mention the incident to anyone.

'The poor, silly fellow was dreadfully distressed for he felt convinced that he would have to carry out this disagreeable command. At the same time he was quite unable to keep the secret to himself and so he divulged the approaching tragedy to his wife.

'The good woman's despair was fully equal to his own, and after much anxious domestic counsel they determined to seek the good offices of a White Witch with the hope that her incantations might overcome the evil spells of the Black Witch who was causing all the mischief. This White Witch prescribed lengthy fasting and other preparations for the great ordeal and, on a given night, she and the bewitched householder, together with his wife and four or five trusty friends, each one with a trusty sword, shut themselves up in a room and commenced their mysterious ceremonial.

'There followed the boiling of occult herbs; the roasting of a beeve's heart stuck full of nails; the reading of certain passages from the family Bible; a mighty display with their swords which were first thrust up the chimney to prevent the Black Witch from coming down after which they were pointed earthward, to prevent Him from rising up. And so this ridiculous "game" continued.

'The only person to benefit, of course, was the imposter who was paid for her services ...'

While the Gazette adds that there had been other Islanders who had been duped over the years, the author added that this should serve as a warning to all Islanders not to believe that they or their animals had been cursed. It was a warning that Trinity's Philip Rondel, in 1930, chose to ignore. But Jersey wasn't the only Island where unscrupulous 'wizards' or 'witches' plied their trade.

As we will see, in the 20th century, in Guernsey, the Quéripel family also used the remnants of superstition to earn money. But was this witchcraft? No, in today's terms it was simply extortion based on the fears of innocent people.

Meanwhile, before moving away from this chapter, one underlying, half-forgotten point needs to be made.

A proverb that could easily have been known in the 16th century runs that 'there's no smoke without fire' and, to put it properly into context, it seems pertinent to add that 'there aren't witch trials without witches'.

However, it must be repeated that there is a huge difference between co-called 'witches' and 'Satanists'. Both existed before Presbyterianism took a tight grip on the Islands' way of life and both existed afterwards. Many of both were destroyed by the courts during the 16th and 17th centuries but just because the last witch was officially executed in 1660 doesn't mean that with her death they had all been wiped out. Far from it.

As the civil powers of Presbyterianism died and a more relaxed form of Christianity eased its way into Island life, evidence of the existence of witches or Satanists began to depend on hand-me-down tales and stories like those told in the Gazette. However, occult practices did continue; and although the next chapter is a collection of some of the more entertaining folklore of the 18th and 19th centuries, it captures the mood of Islanders swathed in superstition, Islanders always fearful of bad omens and their neighbours who, they believed, could never be trusted.

CHAPTER 8

FOLKLORE

A HUNDRED years of witch-hunting were over and Channel Island witch trials were allowed to fade into obscurity. But sorcery is not a craft which appreciates a great deal of publicity, so for the two centuries after trials and persecution came to an end a great deal of the information we have about Island witchcraft is clouded and fragmentary.

However, it should not be imagined that when the last 'witch' was executed and the last of an eccentric breed was eliminated, tales of how such people lived and what they got up too completely disappeared.

The occasional passing comment in a diary, a court record or a parish account also help to paint a picture of the occult in the Islands, and although Victorian writers in particular have embellished witch stories with their own fanciful ideas, beneath many of them are elements which are quite important in this study.

For in many of the stories is another implicit belief – that if there is no rational reason for the event, then the only explanation left must lie in the supernatural. Similarly, some Islanders believed that if things were going wrong for no apparent reason, and if all orthodox attempts to make them better had failed, then why not try a magic charm or two to see if they had any better effect?

At a different, slightly more sinister level, a few Islanders took this idea of the Fates conspiring against them a stage further. When life took an even more dramatic turn for the worse, when illness struck or crops failed, then the idea might creep into your head that someone, somewhere, was conspiring against you. This terrible fear that a member of the community was busy casting spells in your direction was a very real one. It had been present in the witch trials era, just as it continued through the 18th and 19th centuries and traces of it still linger to this day.

The notion is that you start to look suspiciously at your neighbour if misfortune comes your way, for why else would it be there?

Islanders have often been wary of the foreigner (remember that a high proportion of all those tried for witchcraft were outsiders), and this inborn suspicion, combined with a superstitious nature, shows through in most witch stories.

Most would be fables, but they tell us a great deal about the people who used to live in the Islands, while the stories themselves should not be dismissed out of hand. For once they have been dissected and their bare bones examined, if nothing else they are as interesting and entertaining today as they would have been then, at a time when there weren't televisions, films, DVDs and the internet. And some of the stories might even contain an element of truth ... not least because even today some people are suspicious of other people or absolutely hate their neighbours.

At another level, it is obvious that if you don't wash or change your underwear and outer clothing enough, fleas and other vermin might be attracted towards you ... but the credulous might still ask: 'Why me and not the rest of my family?' So the casting of spells alleged to cause lice or similar pests to appear suddenly on the body are very common features of Island tales involving 'sorcery'. But most witnesses to the sorcerer's supposed power to create life from thin air are long gone. Also, modern standards of hygiene make infestation a rare phenomenon and science has undermined the idea that creatures can suddenly and spontaneously appear. Even so, 'suspicion' rather than 'superstition' is a word as common now as it ever was 200 years ago.

But this chapter is not meant to be a philosophical lecture. Instead, it presents a selection of the many folk tales which relate to the past few centuries. Are any of them true? Well, it is up to the reader to make up his or her own mind.

ABOUT the end of the 18th century there lived in Sark a notorious wizard called Pierre de Carteret. He was known locally as 'le vieux diable' and worked only at night, when he employed small devils to help him. If any fishermen passed his house they could hear him working while talking to his helpers in a language they couldn't understand. This is not surprising, for it was the Devil's language he talked.

He built a boat in a barn one morning and the Serquiaise watched in amazement as he launched it at Creux Harbour. How he had managed to get it into the water they never knew, because the barn was far from the sea, and the boat much too large to get through the door. They decided that he had used black magic ...

Because Pierre had no workmen to pay be became very rich. His first wife had also been very wealthy but he was cruel to her, and destroyed her furniture. For instance, he brought his horse into her room and let it kick the place to bits. Soon she was to die of a broken heart.

Pierre married again. His second wife was little more than a child, but a local girl, and when she gave birth to a daughter, called Betsy, she was tutored in the hidden arts and used to feed the cow at night in the churchyard. It always looked healthy and well-fed but no-one would buy butter or milk from the de Carteret family because they knew how it had been produced.

After Pierre's death pictures resembling the Devil were found in his house, which the Sark community quickly burnt. He had been excessively bad in life and had even helped to smuggle ammunition to the French to help them fight the English. On his death no-one grieved, not even his daughter, Betsy.

Pierre de Carteret was, according to legend, a bad man, but there is no tangible proof that he dabbled in sorcery. Instead it could be argued that because he enjoyed his own company better than others, because he was rich and because he married someone a great deal younger than himself, he was shunned and despised. Suspicion, greed and envy are not far from the surface in a tale like this. Like the murdered Elizabet Gavey in Trinity, Pierre was treated suspiciously and was always an outsider.

People were frightened of Elizabeth ... and how many people would have spat on her shadow as she passed to prevent her curses from working? And how many people placed a witch bottle above their doors to prevent her entering their home?

In Guernsey, the Pipet family were also outsiders, treated with suspicion and believed to be witches. In Redstone's 'Guernsey and Jersey Guide' by Louise Lane and published originally in 1843, the authoress writes: 'On the road past St Andrew's church, one of the lanes to the right leads to the village called "Le Hurel" (rocky ground), a collection of mere huts; rude, dirty looking cottages, but remarkable from the people who tenant it. They are a kind of half-gipsy, half-beggar race, bearing the name of Pipet; and kept totally distinct from every other family, because no person would inter-marry with them upon any consideration.

'Their appearance and features are quite unlike the rest of the Guernsey peasantry, who are extremely good-looking, clean, and active; whereas those Pipets may be found basking in the sun, with anything but a prepossessing exterior. The country people consider them as wizards and witches and, at certain times of the year, about Christmas, when they are privileged to go round and beg for their 'Noel' or 'irvières' (New Year's gifts), no-one likes to send them away empty handed for the fear of the consequences to themselves, their cattle, or their children.

'The country people have a great dread of "les Pipaux".'

Marie Pipet was particularly feared. Stories in which she pre-vented meat from roasting or corn from grinding because she was refused favour were well known in St Pierre-du-Bois, and when she wasn't doing mischief, she could be seen in the fields in her other guise of a red-legged chough.

Like all witches she had the power to transform herself into a bird or animal (so the story goes) and this was the shape she liked to adopt. Her neighbours knew this. So, when one morning a small bird, with a ruddy tint to her legs, was discovered in a cow-shed in the parish, tormenting the cattle, the farmhand-in-charge had no hesitation in picking up his pitchfork and running it through the bird's thigh before she could escape.

The day afterwards there was no sign of Marie Pipet until one of her family mentioned that she was in bed, where she was to remain for several months – because of a mysterious leg wound. The neigh-bours nodded their heads and smiled inwardly. They knew about the injury's cause.

How thin the pitchfork had been or how wide the bird's thigh was we are not told, and the latter part of the story is, to say the least, a bit far-fetched; but like the de Carteret family in the tale be-fore, the Pipets did exist – and Marie was later given a proper Christian burial, which helps to dampen any suspicion that she was a malicious devilmonger. The Pipet family name can still be found in Guernsey, just as the Le Brun family name is commonplace in Jersey, where our next story originates.

WELL over a hundred years ago Jean Le Brun was a wealthy farmer, well-liked by his fellow Trinity parishioners and, in turn, he was kindly towards them.

There was one exception, however, for he refused to be pleasant towards Collas de la Fosse, a beggar man, who (so it was believed) had attended a Sabbat on more than one occasion.

One day Collas called at Jean Le Brun's farm to beg for a cup of cider.

'Fiche me l'camp mon vacibond' he was told. But Collas didn't want to go. He also knew that, on the following Saturday, his reluctant host had to walk into town to pass an important contract at the Royal Court and that he, Collas, could prevent him from ever arriving.

So, his reply of 'cidre ou contrat (cider or contract)' should have warned Jean that something nasty was in the offing. Instead, the Trinity farmer pushed Collas away, ignoring his final warning that 'si ou'n'me donnez pon d'cidre, ou's' est fichu d'aller à la Cour samedi. (If you do not give me cider, you will not go to Court on Saturday).'

Jean told of the encounter the next day to some of his neighbours, who tried to warn him that de la Fosse didn't make idle threats, but come Saturday morning an unconcerned Jean Le Brun set out for St Helier.

He never got there. Instead, at the top of Mont Cochon he began to itch.

The itching became worse and, as he looked down at his beautifully tailored coat it seemed to have a life of its own. It was riddled with lice. Le Brun wrenched his collar away, scratched his skin like a man insane, and leapt around in an effort to shake off the devilish vermin. But it was all in vain.

Only after he had turned round and raced back across the fields towards his house did the itching stop, and it wasn't until he was safely behind the front door that the last louse disappeared. Collas de la Fosse's prophecy had come true: Jean Le Brun never did arrive at Court on that Saturday morning.

This is a friendly little tale compared with others involving vermin, and the way that it has become more and more detailed in its handing down, from one generation to another (note how dialogue has been added to it), suggests that, somewhere along the line, a 19th century storyteller has got to work on it. The same, though, cannot be said of the following tale, slight as it is.

The story comes from Guernsey, towards the end of the 19th century, when two female members of the Mauger family plus a friend were attending a dance in one of the outlying parishes.

A rather unpleasant-looking man approached and asked for a dance. The girls refused, which didn't please the man, who walked away muttering something about making the girls suffer.

A minute or two later one of the girls noticed something crawling on her sister's lace collar. It was some sort of maggot.

She killed it, but as she did so many more appeared, and then she noticed that her own gown was similarly riddled with these ugly vermin.

All three girls were soon scratching and itching as they attempted to rid themselves of the wretched things, but it was another three days before they left and then, when they finally disappeared, it was as if they had vanished into thin air.

Of course there could be many reasons why insects suddenly appear in your clothing; not least because you have come into contact with someone whose body and clothing are already riddled by them. But, according to the late George Le Feuvre, writing in the Jersey Evening Post on 14 January, 1984, vermin created by a sorcerer were not body lice as we would know them. They had a look and a texture all of their own.

He also tells how it is possible to make them disappear before the usual three-day infestation period is over. Place a few of them in a saucepan, fry them, and they will all melt away as quickly as they came.

TURNING to a 'sorcerer' must have been good business for Islanders who would take full advantage of superstitious neighbours, although the Vazon 'wizard', Collas Roussell, earned more than he bargained for when he was hauled up in front of the court early in the 18th century for taking money from Guernsey farmers who used him to predict their future. For throwing 'les p'tits bouais' (small sticks or bones, which are thrown to the ground and, depending on how they land, 'read' to predict a customer's fortunes), he was put in the cage in Market Street as a warning to others.

Apparently the Court's warning went unheeded, for in February, 1837, Louis d'Orleans was arrested after admitting that he had extorted money in a similar manner. Not only was Louis prepared to predict a client's future, he was also prepared to change it, if it was within his power. For this extra service, of course, he required greater financial reward. After he had been judged guilty he was sentenced to an hour in the cage in the Market Place and then banished from the Island for six years.

FINALLY, to end this chapter with a touch of true Channel Island whimsy, spare a thought for one Guernseyman who went to a clairvoyant, late in the 19th century, only to be told that he hadn't long to live and that his death would involve a combination of hanging, drowning and burning.

Not surprisingly the man found this very hard to believe and scoffed at the news. He should have known better.

One night, some time later, he was sitting at home, dozing in front of the fire, when it went out. For some reason he had no tinder box and ran to the nearest house to beg a light. His neighbours kindly provided him with a lighted torch and, after thanking them, he set off home as quickly as he could. On his return journey, torch in hand, he attempted to jump a ditch and failed, miserably.

His foot became entangled in some bushes, his head somehow tipped towards the water in the ditch below, and no matter how hard he struggled, each movement only made his position worse. He was stuck fast.

As he dangled there, wondering what on earth would happen next, the torch he had been carrying touched his clothes and set him on fire. In those last, fatal seconds, as his mouth filled up with

'His death would be by hanging, drowning and burning'

muddy water and drowned his screams, it must have been small consolation that the clairvoyant was right for, choked, burnt, and hanging from a thicket, he died.

PART 3
CHAPTER 1
THE 20TH AND 21ST CENTURIES

AS we reach the 20th century our understanding of Channel Island witchcraft changes.

Proof that it existed, and continues to exist, is easier to find, if only because of the number of exorcisms carried out, and although there will always be a thin line between fact and fancy in such an awkward subject, newspaper reports, written statements and real-life witnesses help to bring the story up to date.

In one sense, therefore, Part 3 is about the Islands today. In another sense it is a continuation of Islanders' natural leaning towards the supernatural which has been with them since the earliest times. Although over the centuries pagan beliefs have been swamped by Christianity and the ritual which was practised in the Islands when they were first inhabited has long been forgotten, people don't change: and, until a few years ago, most Channel Islanders were from the same stock who lived alongside the de Carterets in the 16th century; who fought alongside William the Conqueror in 1066; who arrived with William Longsword in 933AD; or who were originally Celts at a time when Christ was only a name on the tongues of a few zealous saints.

Over the centuries, of course, strangers have arrived and made their homes in the Islands, including Huguenots fleeing Catholic persecution, but it has really been only over the past 150 years or so that the Islanders' timeless way of life has been threatened from within, as more and more English people have made the Channel Islands their home. Alderney is a prime example of an island which is far more English now than it would have been 200 years ago.

And, as people arrive and settle they bring new knowledge with them. Nowadays there is more information available than ever about necromancy, magic, eastern mysticism and Wicca, and to a few new Islanders, who try to intellectualise the old beliefs, traditional grimoires must seem sadly out-dated. In certain parishes, however, the newcomers have not infiltrated the community to such an extent that a Channel Islander who, if taken back in time to a bygone age, wouldn't have immediately felt at home.

In certain farmhouses, in St Ouen or St Pierre-du-Bois, for example, families with a long pedigree and an equally long memory are resistant to change and the fisherman son will still cross himself as he goes past certain rocks to ward off evil spirits, as his ancestors did before him: or the farmer will still remember playing a game of tag when he was a child in which the catcher was called 'le djablle' (the Devil) and the area to which he took his prisoners was called 'Enfier' (Hell).

The same farmer will also think twice about going past a witch's rock at night, especially on Candlemas Day (2 February), Lammas (1 August), St Thomas's Day (21 December) and the Eve of St John (23 June), for he knows that if he does so he might meet a coven of witches. At one time he might have known all of them as friends or neighbours, but not any more – newcomers get everywhere.

Meanwhile, the Islands are still inhabited by people like Collas Roussel or Louis d'Orleans, mentioned in the last chapter, people who say that they have the power to look into the future and who prefer to operate on their own. Some of them we would call white witches and they are either consulted – as they have always been – or they are shunned – as they have always been – because people are afraid that as well as a magical sixth sense which can be turned to your advantage they also have the power to bring you face-to-face with personal tragedy.

White witches or black, both need to be treated with the greatest respect; and the idea of a witch's curse should not be treated lightly. This is also true in Normandy, which has a witch history not unlike our own. In 'Croyances et Traditions Populaires en Normandie' (The Department of La Manche, No. 25, 1983), for example, there are several stories of 'la sorcellérie', any of which could easily belong to the Channel Islands. One, in particular, has echoes of our dear old friend, the 18th century sorcerer of St Brelade.

In the Norman story, said to have happened earlier this century, a wicked witch was trapped when a cauldron full of chickweed was stirred for about half an hour by two strong men, who also read a passage from an old grimoire as they stirred. After 27 minutes or so the witch (who had cast a particularly nasty spell on a farmer and his cattle) was suddenly revealed to the hard-done-by farmer, who demanded compensation

Compared with the 1787 story from the Gazette, chickweed seems so much tastier than an ox's heart cooked in urine.

So much for France. But what was happening in Guernsey at the turn of the century?

GUERNSEY

IN December, 1902, Dr Laurie Robinson was having problems with the friends of one of his patients. Writing to Miss Edith Carey from Melrose on 11 December that year, the Doctor recalls: A patient of mine at St Pierre-du-Bois suffered from an affection of the brain which has led to a total loss of sight.

It was supposed by the wise people around her that she was suffering from 'mal volant', so a black fowl was waved three times round her head on three successive days to the accompaniment of a prayer. On the ninth day the fowl ought to have died and the woman recovered. As this did not happen they concluded that their diagnosis was wrong.

As the Reverend Thomas Brock before him, the good doctor had discovered that his neighbours in the parish were highly superstitious and quite prepared to turn to magic when all conventional medicines had failed.

Fortunately, because he was not involved with the ritual, and because the only harm had been done to a confused and dizzy hen, Dr Robinson was able to laugh off the action of these rival practitioners and he bore them no ill-will.

This might not have been the case if one of his patients had been Mr Wilson Bréhaut of St Peter and his four children, Clifford, Henry, Amy and Lena.

For the Bréhaut children were lousy and, according to their father, sorcery was the cause of their verminous condition. In the Guernsey Evening Press for 9 May, 1912, under the headline 'Alleged sorcery', the whole sad story is revealed.

Apparently, the head of St Peter's School, Mr C. J. H. Rawlinson, had tried on several occasions to persuade Mr Bréhaut to delouse his children and to send them to school in clean clothes.

Bréhaut refused; and he and his wife spent a great deal of time explaining that the lice had nothing to do with them, ascribing the condition of their children to jealousy on the part of their neighbours. Their children had been bewitched, they said, and they were powerless to do anything in the face of malevolent sorcery.

Bréhaut even appealed to the Bailiff, Sir William Carey, asking him what was he to do against a sorcerer's curse. But the Bailiff was sceptical about the whole affair, seemed to have little faith in sorcery, and suggested that what the children really needed was a good scrub in soap and water.

Despite Bréhaut's insistence that a Constable at the Islets was ready to swear that 'the presence of the vermin was brought about by jealous persons' and that his neighbours had access to 'little books' on the subject, which had been bought in France, he was fined two shillings and six pence and ordered to send his children to school in a clean condition.

As the Bailiff left the Court after fining Bréhaut, probably shaking his head as he did so and thinking of the extraordinary lengths to which some people would go to avoid taking a bath, he wasn't to know that there was an even more sinister witch trial in the offing. For if Bréhaut genuinely believed that his children had been infested with lice through the ill-will of his neighbours, spare a thought for Mrs Houton, from St Martin.

While Clifford, Henry, Amy et al were being deloused, she was close to being literally scared to death.

THE trial against Mrs Amy Henrietta Lake for 'exercé le metier de dire la bonne aventure et exercé l'art prétendu de la sorcellerie' was fully reported in the Guernsey Star on Thursday, 29 January 1914, but the events leading up to the trial go back at least a year.

Mrs Lake was a 'witch' (and not a very nice one, either) and she had become involved with Mrs Houtin, who kept a farm at the Croute Fallaize, St Martin, in October 1913. In that month Mrs Houtin went to the defendant's house because her cattle were ill, and she believed that a spell had been placed upon them. Mrs Lake told her she was wise to visit her and that she was right about the spell – adding that her visitor's husband, who had recently died, had also been under a spell and that this had killed him.

While this titbit of information was fresh in Mrs Houtin's ears, Mrs Lake continued talking to her new-found friend, saying that a similar spell had been placed upon her and that she needed help if she wasn't to go the same way as her cows and her late husband, but, after so much bad news, Mrs Lake assured a rather devastated Mrs Houtin that help was at hand.

For just 15 francs she would reveal the identity of the sorcerer and provide salts to destroy the sorcerer power. She would also provide some powders which, when burnt, would help cure a headache Mrs Houtin had had for several months. Numbed by this information, Mrs Houtin paid and, after following Mrs Lake's careful instructions, found that her headache did go away after the salts had been thrown and the powders burnt. Unfortunately, she also discovered that she needed repeat prescriptions, which kept going up in price.

The costs eventually became too much for her: she could no longer afford Mrs Lake's services, which did not please the Guernsey sorceress. She explained to her client that, unless she was paid £3 within the next few days, she would be dead by 23 January. Not unnaturally, this upset poor Mrs Houtin, 'who took elaborate precautions to ward off the 'evil eye', but without much success. She became so ill that for three days she had to stay in bed while her daughter nursed her; she was 'as helpless as a child'.

By 16 January and with only a week to go before her expected death, Mrs Houtin was desperate enough to call in the police. At this stage of the court proceedings P.C. Adams was asked to explain his role in the drama. At 6.30 p.m. on 16 January, he said, he had been called to the harbourmaster's office in St Sampson's, where he had found Mrs Houtin in an agitated state.

In a confused manner she told him that a witch had placed a spell upon her and if she did not pay £3 to Mrs Lake by the following Friday, she would die within the next week. The case, of course, was brought to trial after this date, so when His Majesty's Comptroller pointed out that 'she was living still' the court burst into laughter – which had to be silenced before P.C. Adams continued making his statement. He explained that at the time Mrs Houtin was in such a poor state of mind he would not have been surprised if she had committed suicide before she got home. He had advised her to see Canon Foran, and she did so.

Canon Foran confirmed P.C. Adam's testimony, and told the court that Mrs Houtin had decided to visit him. He had listened to her story with sympathy and advised her to go home and say her prayers, after which the power of the evil eye would be cast off. Since offering this advice, he had not seen the woman.

The day after Mrs Houtin visited the good churchman, police constables Adams and Lihou visited her at her home and took her statement. They then went into the garden and dug up a number of packets of powder, which had been buried at a depth of about 2 ft 'at the cardinal points of the compass'.

The powders consisted of Brown and Poulson's flour, Paisley flour, brown starch and baking powder. After finding these magical, calorie-enriched ingredients, they began to call upon other clients who had dealt with Mrs Lake, including Joseph Orphelin, who had paid £7 10 shillings for some charms, and Marie Roger, who had paid £3 10 shillings in return for some advice and a ring, which she had been assured would keep away any evil spells from her home. Another young woman, Felicité Garnier, swore that she had heard Mrs Lake warn Mrs Ophelin that she was bewitched, and that to counteract the spell she would have to burn certain powders.

P.C. Lihou confirmed that all of the people mentioned above had been in contact with Mrs Lake, adding that when Mrs Houtin had been asked to touch a box of powders, discovered in a farm outhouse, she had refused, saying it was 'full of little devils'. Understandably, the court found the charge proved. Mrs Lake was sentenced to the full penalty available for the crime, which was eight days' imprisonment.

The sentence was hardly long enough, according to His Majesty's Procureur, who explained that because the maximum penalty for such a crime was so light, Crown Officers were making arrangements to bring forward a proposal to make the offence punishable by a longer term of imprisonment. (In 1915 a new law was added to the statute books in Guernsey. For 'exercising the false art of sorcery' it was possible that a 'witch' could go to jail for up to two years, with or without hard labour. (In 1982 this was repealed and nowadays the same offence would carry a fine of up to £100, two months imprisonment, or both.)

After arrangements had been made to look after Mrs Lake's children during her stay in prison, she was led to the cells.

The court case had caused a sensation in the Island. It was followed by a stern rebuke in the Star that the evils of sorcery were more widespread than most people believed (the same thing the Jersey Gazette had said over 100 years before) and that 'the recent case is mild and innocent in comparison with some that might be brought forward were it not for the difficulty of obtaining sufficient proof and witnesses to satisfy a court of law'.

Reluctant to let an opportunity pass when the leader writers could get their teeth into something with real flesh on it, the paper continued: 'The numbers of those victimised during the past few years might probably be reckoned by the hundred; fear, suspicion, ill-will, the sundering of friendships and the estrangement of relations, the impoverishment of families, even sickness caused by terror alone, have been some of the faults of a system born of the rapacity of these vampires (i.e. witches) and the readiness of the foolish to believe the most absurd and impossible stories when backed by a claim of supernatural powers.'

The Star: 5 February 1914

IT was all heady stuff, but the case against Mrs Lake is interesting for two further reasons. First is the Procureur's concern about the maximum penalty available to the court at the end of the trial. It was trivial, compared with the degree of suffering that Mrs Houtin had endured; 300 years before, Mrs Lake would have gone to the stake for the wicked way she had manipulated her neighbours' fears; now the punishment was either a fine or eight days in jail. It would seem that the court's powers had gone from one extreme to another – 17th century sorcerers were executed, but in the 20th century it was difficult enough to find a law by which they could be tried, let alone convict them. The second point of interest relates to Mrs Lake's maiden name. It was Quéripel. Remembering that sorcery is supposed to run in families, it is well worth looking back at the court records of 4 November, 1598 and 22 October, 1624.

On that first date Alichette Quéripel, wife of Pierre Rolland of St Andrew, was burnt at the stake for witchcraft, and on the second date her son, Jean, was similarly punished. If anything can emphasise the timeless quality of Island life (and witchcraft) it ought to be this 300-year connection between a Guernsey family and its descendants. Sadly, however, for all of the Quéripel involvement with devil-mongery, they had not improved their fortunes by the early years of the 20th century and Amy's name is mentioned more than once in court records after her conviction for sorcery for offences which have nothing to do with witchcraft.

Her husband, Walter John Lake, is also mentioned – mainly for violence against his mother and wife.

JERSEY

THIS account is from the Evening Post's letter pages of 1932: 'Dear Sir, Since coming to Jersey I have been greatly surprised at the superstitions of some of the people here who otherwise appear quite sane.

'They fully believe in witchcraft, spells, charms and the evil eye. Aches, pains or even simple warts, they must go to the charmer, who is generally some dirty old man or woman. As far as I can gather, the only thing he seems to charm from them is his fee.

'Now, if local preachers could only be induced to say a few words against this practice, I am sure it would soon disappear.

'Yours faithfully,

'W Butler,

'La Robeline, St Ouen.'

THERE are those who dabble in black magic, some of whom do so merely to bring excitement into their lives. Others have the serious intention of trying to harm those who stand in their way or whom they dislike, but black magic has a mysterious way of rebounding on them – as in the case of Rollo Ahmed, whose case went to the courts, as we have already seen, in 1930.

But there is a darker side to these Islands – superstition, devil worship ... call it what you will; for 30 times during the 1980s Guernsey's exorcist, appointed by the Bishop of Winchester, was called out to various homes without publicity and usually to include, as part of the exorcism, Holy Communion. Jersey's 2013 exorcist has also been called out on various occasions.

ON Monday, 13 December, 1971, Edward John Louis Paisnel was sentenced to 30 years' imprisonment on 13 charges connected with attacks on seven people living in Jersey, including the rape of a 14-year-old girl in 1960 and attempted sodomy with an 11-year-old boy in 1970.

The full number of boys and girls sexually assaulted by Paisnel after 1960 (and perhaps before) will never be known because of a natural reluctance by many of the victims to go to the police. In his summing-up at the end of the trial, the Attorney-General, Peter Crill, on behalf of the prosecution, said: 'I do not know the motive behind these assaults, but although much has been written in the popular press about black magic, this has never been part of the case of the defence.'

This is true, but Ted Paisnel said he had been involved with witchcraft since 1949 and that as his life became more perverse, he had sunk deeper and deeper into Satanism. There is also evidence enough to show that he worshipped the Devil or justified his crimes through Satan and what he believed to be his family background.

He was, for example, proud of the fact that in the 15th century the terrible Satanist Gilles de Rais had been engaged to a member of the Paisnel family – young Jeanne Paisnel – when she was only 12. Gilles de Rais went on to become one of the most influential military leaders in France and helped Joan of Arc rid the country of English forces during the Hundred Years War. Towards the end of his life, however, he became a monster, turned to black magic and bestiality of the worst kind and was alleged to have abused and killed over 300 youngsters before he, in turn, was executed after being arrested by the French authorities in October 1440.

He was, by all accounts, a terrible man who deserved punish-

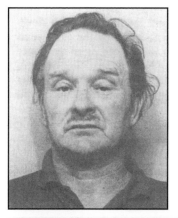

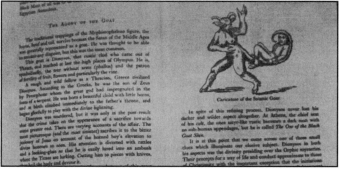

**Edward Paisnel, the 'Beast of Jersey' (top left) and two of the
Demonologie books found in his possession**
(pictures courtesy of the Reverend Robert Law)

ment but the connection between the Baron and Ted Paisnel was
tenuous, to say the least.

More incriminating in the eyes of the Jersey police was Paisnel's
reaction to a raffia crucifix, found in the glove compartment of a
stolen car he was driving on 10 July, the day of his arrest in 1971.
When Paisnel was shown the raffia cross at the police station, after
he had been taken there with other contents of the car, including a
gruesome face-mask, wig, gloves and a large blue coat with inch-
long nails protruding from the shoulders and lapels, he 'almost

jumped over the table', according to Detective Sergeant John Marsh of the CID. 'His eyes nearly popped out of his head, his face went a deep red and he began to chuckle in a strange manner. Then he declared "My Master would laugh very long and loud at this".

The raffia cross was the property of the daughter of the car's owner, and had been made for a school nativity play – but Paisnel wasn't to know this.

He did, however, know how the rest of the strange equipment had got into the Morris 1100 he had stolen. He had put it there. To even the most trusting of policemen it was obvious that Paisnel had something to hide and, as the questioning continued, Detective Sergeant Colin Lang casually pointed to the crucifix again and asked: 'Are you afraid of the cross?'

To which Paisnel replied that he wasn't, while adding 'there's a much more powerful emblem than that'. He refused to touch the cross when it was handed to him, commenting brusquely 'your world is shrinking – our cocoon is getting larger', which was hardly the reassuring statement of an innocent man.

Within a short space of time the rest of the Jersey police force knew that at long last the 'Beast of Jersey' had been arrested, but the most damning piece of evidence to link him to devilmongery was yet to come. When the police searched Paisnel's family home, Maison du Soleil in Grouville, they found behind a red curtain in one of the rooms a kind of altar, with a witch's familiar (a china toad), a wooden sacrificial knife, cloves, and a chalice on display. Behind the altar was a hidden room which contained many items linking the accused with the sex crimes of the past ten years. The room itself was odd, having a powerful, musty smell, and nearly everything in it was painted blue.

Among Paisnel's other possessions were discovered books on Satanism, including Eric Maple's 'The Dark World of Witches' and Henry Rhodes's 'The Satanic Mass' – further proof that, at the very least, he was interested in black magic.

Eventually, Ted Paisnel stood trial and was imprisoned and details of his crimes and the evil he perpetrated can be found in 'The Beast of Jersey' by Ward Rutherford.

However, this is a study of the history of witchcraft in the Channel Islands and although Paisnel must figure in the study, his role in history is not as great as one might think. For, if Ted Paisnel had not chosen to hang his evil desires on the peg of witchcraft, he would almost certainly have hung them on some other faith or creed.

The Attorney-General, Peter Crill, realised this. He added the following to the earlier statement made in connection with Paisnel's association with witchcraft: 'If Paisnel was acting out a fantasy ... this has not been borne out by pyschiatrist reports ... This was a man who had deliberately gratified his lust on young children as and when he wished ... He is a cunning and hideous man who appears to show no remorse, horror, or emotion for the crime he has perpetrated.'

Paisnel used Satanism as an excuse to justify his crimes and as a shield to hide behind; and although he may have been known by other Channel Island witches he was not typical of that breed; he was also a loner and, if he did claim to have magical powers, they were not able to save him from the powers of the law.

If he had been born 50 or 70 years earlier, however, he might have been able to learn a lot more about witchcraft from two covens, one of which, it is believed, met at No.12, Beresford Street, St Helier, the other at The Homestead, St Lawrence.

What is believed to have been a witches' temple in Beresford Street came to light only towards the end of the 20th century. On 5 November, 1981, its discovery and appearance were described in the Jersey Evening Post. Marked out on the floor of a secret room in a property known as Leetian Health Foods was a magical circle with green, cream and red symbols painted around it.

The symbols included six-pointed stars, tulips (supposedly connected with fertility rites) and an anvil – labelled by one student of the occult as a 'representation of the gateway to Satan'. The boards were given to La Société Jersiaise, although the owner of the house was advised to have them exorcised and then burnt.

The temple thought to have existed in The Homestead was, if anything, more alarming than the one discovered in Beresford Street because of its chilly atmosphere. In even the warmest weather it was supposed to have remained many degrees colder

Lee Ryan and the 'magic circle' discovered at what, at the time, was Leetian Health Foods, Beresford Street (1981)

than the rest of the house and the space, measuring about 3 ft by 9 ft, seemed tainted by evil. The house itself has a history of unhappiness and of poltergeist activity and haunting. It is to be hoped that that evil reputation has now disappeared – it was exorcised two decades ago.

Witchcraft, in various forms, still exists in Jersey and even now Islanders ask for the services of an exorcist. As late as September, 1982 the Reverend Robert Law conducted a service of Holy Communion in the room of a so-called witch who lived in the west of the Island.

CHAPTER 2
LEY LINES

ARTHUR Watkins never lived to see the full effect of his book 'The Old Straight Path'. When he wrote it in 1925 it seemed innocuous enough; all he was trying to prove was that stone monuments were arranged in distinct patterns reaching for miles across the countryside in precise straight lines.

Along that line might be found a Neolithic stone circle, an early Christian church or a similar building on the site of some former prehistoric creation. In effect he was suggesting that our ancestors had been building lines of communication stretching across the length and breadth of Europe.

Watkins tried to prove his theory by showing on ordnance survey maps how easy it is to go from one stone monument to another, then to another, and so on, always keeping a straight line as each stone building is reached. Surely, he concluded, it was no coincidence that so may dolmens, menhirs and other stone artefacts had been placed in such an organised way.

The trouble is, of course, if Arthur Watkins was correct, what were the straight lines for?

As Aubrey Burl explained in 'Rings of Stone' (published by Francis Lincoln, London, 1979) in a damaging chapter entitled 'Lunacy, Leys and Legends', the notion of ley-lines as 'old straight tracks' is hardly practicable.

If early man had tried to walk in a straight line between one dolmen and another he would have had to find a way across the roughest of waterfalls, climb the steepest of cliffs, and leap across the widest of ravines.

Dismissing Watkins's suggestion as 'the most lunatic of ideas', Burl concluded that if stone monuments were built as beacons, marking out a system of pathways, then prehistoric people must have been unbelievably stupid in their choice of routes.

But the idea of leys caught on and members of 'The Straight Track Club' and their friends weren't to be dissuaded.

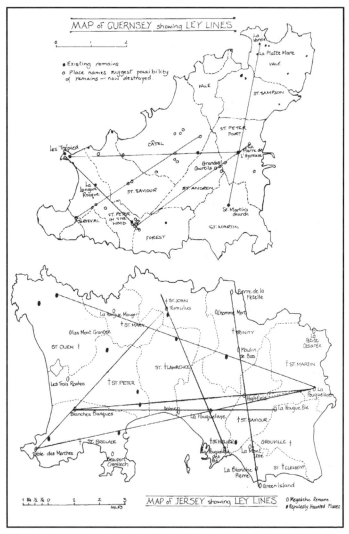

**More than one critic has dismissed entirely Arthur Watkins'
suggestion that ley lines exist and that they possess some
kind of mystical force that can be tapped into. But who
determines the rules?**

In 1969, for example, Guy Underwood, one of Watkins's admirers, suggested in 'Pattern of the Past' that stone age tombs were traversed by some kind of current and were, in a sense, 'live'.

In other words, Neolithic monuments are spiritual generators linked to each other by psychic energy radiating across the countryside in a network of invisible rays ... lines of kinetic force, emanating from the forgotten, extra-sensory powers of a prehistoric people. In less jargonistic terms stone circles are a kind of weird, supernatural telephone service between us and our predecessors.

Certainly a Mrs Smithett (in 'Earth Magic' by Francis Hitching, Cassell, 1976) feels that there is something in this because, 'there is a definite change in the feeling of a stone circle after dusk. The power seems quite different'.

Other people have felt something untoward emanating from these prehistoric stone monuments.

In the foothills of the Wicklow mountains in Ireland lies an ancient stone circle where squat granite rocks remind locals of legends connected with sun-worship and human sacrifice. On one of these stones, years ago, someone carved a Christian cross to exorcise the evil that lingered there and to counteract any truth behind the 1,000-year-old rhyme, preserving the legend of sacrifice:

'Their god was he –
That Cromm, all misty, withered, wan –
Those whom he ruled so fearfully –
Are dead – and whither have they gone?
To him – oh, shame!
Their children, piteous babes, they slew,
Their blood they poured out in his name,
With wailing cries, and tears, and rue.'

SO much for Ireland and the powers that may or may not live in the stone circle at Wicklow. But what about the Channel Islands, which have many similarities with the Emerald Isle, and are ripe with ancient standing stones all their own?

One of the Islands' most famous dolmens is at Faldouet, in St Martin, Jersey. In late 1982, people living near the dolmen complained to a local clergyman that their houses were cold, and that

**An old picture of an 'altar of sacrifice' in the Islands ...
possibly on a Jersey ley line?**

they felt they had been invaded by something evil. The clergyman, who was also the local diocesan exorcist, was asked if he could give an explanation.

He did his best. He explained that their homes were on a ley-line running west from the dolmen and that more than once in recent years, to the best of his knowledge, some sort of power had been guided along that ley-line. If that explanation didn't satisfy the householders, the clergyman could have explained further.

In 1981 and then in 1982, he had been called out to the Faldouet dolmen to perform a full-scale exorcism at the Neolithic site. On both occasions there was ample evidence to show that some kind of cult had been active there while, to this day, at different parts of the year various ceremonies take place there. These usually conducted by 'white witches' or the Wicca and, according to at least one of them, are completely harmless as they try to trace their way back in time to an older faith which bears no relationship with Satanism. You know when the stones have been used: rose petals or shells can be found there afterwards.

Some Wiccans are also regular church-goers who believe in the Christian God while also recognising that there were other gods and beliefs before Christ was born.

CHAPTER 3

WICCA: A SOURCE OF GOOD OVER EVIL

RHIANNA Galvin is a fifth-generation Romany gypsy. As well as being a busy mum she is a medium and clairvoyant and also a practising Wicca.

But what exactly does a 21st century 'witch' do to ease away the nations's pains?

Firstly, you have to think about getting up in the morning, which is why she explained: 'I live by the seasons, and I'm very conscious of the planet that we live on and how we live, and very conscious of how I am with other people because we believe in the three-fold law; whatever we send out comes back to us three times. And I am a clairvoyant medium and that's how I work on a daily basis, so hopefully I am helping people.

'And although people might judge me otherwise, I'm just an ordinary housewife, a normal mum who is no different from anyone else, be they politician or lawyer. And I'm certainly guilty of no harm to anyone else who lives in the street. "Wicca" and its followers largely disregard the world around them but are aware of spirituality, which in turn leads to them becoming aware of other things around them, from the media, television, magazines and things like that. And it is also more accepted now ... And yes, I'd like to see the "craft" accepted more and more on 21st century terms, obviously – it's just known about more.

'If you aren't convinced, look again at the Spirit & Destiny magazine, which has opened it up to a broader spectrum and which plays down any of the sensationalisms usually connected with their disease.

'I usually recognise as well that more and more people have bought that and realised what witchcraft is, as opposed to sensationalising it, which can happen sometimes.

'Wicca is very popular among teenage girls in a time where Christianity has been really struggling to get teenagers into the pew; Wicca appeals to a younger generation partly because it's a kinder, more meaningful faith and it's not so dominated, either, by the male patriarchal side of things which can be quite difficult for younger people, across the board, when they are trying to find themselves but soon realise in other religions the men want total control.

'As a medium and clairvoyant I will always try and make contact with people's loved ones who have passed over although I can't guarantee that I am going to do that but I am going to try for them. And that has been a comfort for people, and it really helps them – it's good for them to realise that their loved ones go on. It's not just like nailing a lid on and that's the end of it all – they are still there and they can gain comfort from that.

'If people come here to me and go away feeling happier and lighter and more at ease with everything then I have worked well and I have done my job properly.

'And yes, I can see part of the future but I can't tell people what they should or should not do. That's for them to decide. My role is merely to show them the possibilities of life to come. As for ceremonies ... Halloween is our new year and it's the third of the harvest festivals.

'A very long time ago it would be time when people could relax because all their food would be gathered in for the winter and they would feel safe that they had enough food for themselves and their animals.

'Our faith doesn't permit us to do evil. "Wicca"* is a positive source. Not a negative one. And, if anything, it's a 21st century answer to all the harm that's gone before.'

*WICCA (as defined by Wikipedia) is a modern pagan, witchcraft religion. It was developed in England during the first half of the 20th century and it was introduced to the public in 1952 by Gerald Gardner, a retired British civil servant. It draws upon a diverse set of ancient pagan and 20th century hermetic motifs for its theological structure and ritual practice.

'Wicca is a diverse religion with no central authority or figure defining it. It is divided into various lineages and denominations, referred to as "traditions", each with its own organisational structure and level of centralisation.

'Due to its decentralised nature, there is some disagreement over what actually constitutes Wicca. Some traditions, collectively referred to as British Traditional Wicca, strictly follow the initiatory lineage of Gardner and consider the term "Wicca" to apply only to such lineaged traditions, while other eclectic traditions do not.

'Wicca is typically duo-theistic, worshipping a god and goddess traditionally viewed as a mother goddess and horned god. These two deities are often viewed as facets of a greater pantheistic "hard" polytheism or even monotheism. Wiccan celebration follows approximately eight seasonally based festivals known as "Sabbats".

'Wicca involves the ritual practice of magic.'

CHAPTER 4

THE COURT'S DECISION

JERSEY, October 10, 1591:

'Whereas Symon Vauldin, of the parish of St Brelade, having confessed to having communicated and spoken to the Devil on many occasions, under the form of a cat or crow, and having for long been suspected of the crime of sorcery as well as the said apparitions, and having been subjected to the question of his guilt or innocence, his life or death, to an Enquete du Pays, according to the laws of the country. The said Enquete of 24, having examined their conscience on the action of the said Vauldin, unanimously swore on their soul that they believed that the said Vauldin was a sorcerer who lived a wicked and detestable life. After the Enquete the said Symon Vauldin was condemned to be dressed in a linen surplice, tied to a post and strangled and his body burnt until it be reduced to ashes. All his goods, chattels and property confiscated and forfeited for the Crown and others to whom it should belong.'

(Official Court Records; page 393)

THE following lists show the results of most of the witch trials between 1550 and 1661 and I am indebted to S. Carey Curtis's 'Trials for Witchcraft in Guernsey' in the 1937 edition of 'Transactions of La Société Guernsiaise' for most of the information contained in the first list, and to G.R. Balleine's article in the 1939 'Bullétins' from La Société Jersiaise, which helped me to compile the second.

Balleine is right when he says that the law offered the witch many safeguards against injustice (in Jersey, for example she could challenge hostile jurors, and if five jurors found her not guilty she would be acquitted), but the truth is that if you were accused of witchcraft the taint of sorcery stayed with you for the rest of your life. Christine Ramon discovered this in 1626. She was banished from Guernsey on suspicion of witchcraft in 1617, but returned on 6 May 1626. She was arrested and, on 21 July, she was hanged. So was she a witch, or merely a woman who had nowhere else to go?

There is another problem, for if you were the only person on a jury who believed a suspect was innocent, there was always the possibility that the taint of Satanism might drift your way ... Why side with a witch when everyone else knows he or she's guilty?

And there is another feature of the witch-trials which must be mentioned ... The trials were not pretty affairs, and what makes them less pretty, more gruesome, is the malicious intent shown by Seigneurs and commoners alike.

One of the ways, it would appear, that you could gain revenge on a neighbour was to accuse him, or her, of sorcery. Sometimes it worked – and your neighbour was reduced to ashes, so you didn't have to worry about him any more. Sometimes (and only occasionally, according to contemporary accounts) those people who began the witch-scare by going to their Elders were themselves penalised for gossip-mongering. This happened to Collas Pirouet and his wife, Richard Le Gendre and his wife, in October, 1597.

All four had accused Jersey girl Ann Pirouet of sorcery but, for a change, the court refused to listen. Instead, the magistrate decided that if any of those who had brought the charge against Ann in the first place continued to spread malicious gossip, they would be fined 100 sous at the following court session.

So much for the common touch – but what of the Seigneurs, the Lords of the manor and the parish, who had so much power over the Islands and their people? Despite their avowed Christian intent, their sense of moral outrage seemed to be felt most keenly when they thought they had something to lose, as Jean Dumaresq, of Samarès Manor showed in 1585. He was livid when Jean Morant was sentenced by the Jersey court to be executed at the foot of Mont de St Helier.

'It wasn't fair,' he told the Court: 'It prejudiced the rights of the Seigneur. Jean should be executed at Samarès, where he belongs.' What Dumaresq was really saying was that Jean Morant's possessions belonged to the Seigneur of the fief he used to live in. If he had been executed at Samarès Manor, guess where all of his 'goods, chattels and inherited property' would have gone?

THE COURT'S DECISION
GUERNSEY

Hellier Gosselin, Bailiff

1 June 1550: Jean Thoumes: Executed (no other details).

Thomas Compton, Bailiff

2 August 1563: Colette Gascoing: Whipped at the crossroads. One ear was nailed to the pillory, cut off and thrown into the sea: Banished for life.

3 November 1563: Francoise Regnouff: Burnt at the stake.

4 November 1563: Martin Tulouff: Burnt at the stake.

5 November 1563: Collette Salmon: Burnt at the stake.

6 November 1563: Gracene Gousset: Burnt at the stake.

7 November 1563: Catherine Prays: Burnt at the stake.

8 October 1570: Michelle Tourtel: Burnt at the stake.

9 October 1570: Coliche Tourtel: Banished for 15 years.

10 October 1570: Jeanette du Maresq: Banished for 7 years.

11 October 1570: James de la Rue: Banished for 7 years.

12 November 1570: Lorenche Faleze: Burnt at the stake.

13 November 1570: Thomasse Salmon: Whipped at the cross roads. One ear was nailed to the pillory, cut off and thrown into the sea: Banished.

14 November 1570: Marie Gauvain: As above.

Guillaume de Beauvoir, Bailiff

15 May 1581: Katherine Eustache: Tried; not convicted.

Thomas Wymore, Bailiff

16 March 1583: Collis de la Rue: Released without evidence.

17 May 1586: Collis de la Rue: Fresh trial: Burnt at the stake.

Louis de Vic, Bailiff

18 July 1594: Mayer Martin (alias Salmon): Burnt at the stake.

19 November 1598: Alichette Quéripel: Burnt at the stake.

20 December 1603: Marie Rolland: Burnt at the stake.

21 July 1605: Anne Gruth: Burnt at the stake.

22 July 1605: Pierre Mauger: Burnt at the stake.

23 July 1605: Jeanne le Roux: Burnt at the stake.

24 June 1609: Helleyne Le Brun: Banished for ever.

25 June 1609: Jean Henri: Suspected, but released.

26 June 1613: Ollivier Omont: Burnt at the stake.

27 June 1613: Cecille Vautier: Banished for ever.
(wife of Ollivier Omont)

28 June 1613: Guillemine Omont: Banished for ever.
(Their daughter)

29 July 1613: Laurence L'Eustache: Burnt at the stake.
(wife of Thomas le Compte)

30 July 1617: Collette du Mont: Burnt at the stake.
(widow of John Becquet)

31 July 1617: Marie du Mont: As above.
(daughter of Collette du Mont)

22 July 1617: Isabel Becquet: As above.

33 July 1617: Collis Becquet: Result not recorded.

34 August 1617: Jeanne Guignon: Burnt at the stake.

35 August 1617: Michelle Jervaise: Burnt at the stake.

36 August 1617: Marie Becquet: Banished for ever.

37 August 1617: Aulne Massi: Burnt at the stake.

38 October 1617: Katherine Hamon: Banished.

39 October 1617: Jean de Callais: The entire de Callais
family and their servants were banished for ever.

42 October 1617: Philipine Le Parmentier: Burnt at the stake.

43 November 1617: Christine Hamon: Banished but returned nine
years later.

44 December 1618: Jean Nicolle of Sark: Suspected, banished.

45 May 1619: Pierre Massi: Condemned to be burnt; escaped from
prison and drowned.

46 August 1619: Jeane Béhot of Alderney: Suspected, banished.

47 April 1620: Girette Parmentier: Banished for ever.

48 April 1620: Jeanne Le Cornu: Suspected, banished for ever.

49 May 1622: Collette de L'Etacq: Burnt at the stake.

50 May 1622: Catherine Hallouvris: Result not recorded.

51 May 1622: Collette Robin: Burnt at the stake.

52 October 1622: Etienne Le Compte: Burnt at the stake.

53 October 1622: Jeanne Chivret: Result not recorded.

54 October 1622: Mary Blanche: Burnt at the stake.

55 October 1622: Jean Le Moigne: No evidence, so released.

56 October 1622: Guillemine La Bourse: No evidence, so released.

57 October 1622: Thomas Tourgis: Burnt at the stake.

58 October 1622: Jeane Tourgis: Burnt at the stake.

(Thomas's daughter)

59 October 1622: Michelle Chivrette: Burnt at the stake.

(wife of Pierre Oment)

60 November 1622: Perrine Marest: Suspected, banished for ever.

61 June 1624: Pierre Becquet: Burnt at the stake.

62 June 1624: Ester Henry: Ordered to be burnt alive and her ashes scattered.

63 June 1624: Marguerite Tardif: No evidence, so released.

64 June 1624: Pierre Massi: Burnt at the stake.

(son of Pierre)

65 June 1624: Jean de France: As his wife, above.

66 July 1624: Collette La Gelée: Burnt at the stake

67 October 1624: Jean Quéripel: Burnt at the stake.

68 July 1625: Elizabeth Duquemin: Suspected, banished.

69 April 1626: Judith de France: Accused of sorcery, but result not recorded.

70 May 1626: Christine Hamon: Hanged on 21 July.

71 August 1626: Jeanne de Bertran: Burnt at the stake.

72 August 1626: Marie Sohier: Burnt at the stake.

73 August 1626: Marie de Garis: Burnt at the stake

74 August 1627: Rachel Alexandre: Burnt at the stake.

75 August 1627: Job Nicolle of Sark: Suspected, banished.

76 November 1627: Judith Alexandre: Suspected, banished.

77 January 1629: Anne Blampied: Banished for seven years.

78 January 1629: Thomas Heaume: As above.

79 May 1629: Marguerite Picot: Burnt at the stake.

80 August 1629: Susanne Prud'homme: Burnt at the stake.

81 August 1629: Massi Jéhan: Result not recorded.

82 August 1629: Jacqueline Salmon: Burnt at the stake.

Jean de Quetteville, Bailiff

83 July 1631: Marie Mabile: Burnt at the stake.

84 July 1631: Thomas Chivret: Burnt at the stake.

85 July 1631: Susanne Jouanne: Suspected, banished for ever.

86 July 1631: Four daughters of Susanne and Etienne Le Compte banished for 15 years.

87 October 1631: Marie Moitie: Released because of insufficient evidence.

88 October 1631: Philippe Chivret: Result not recorded.
89 October 1631: Vincente Canu: Released because of insufficient evidence.

90 October 1631: Jéhan Nicolle of Sark: Result not recorded.

91 October 1631: Marie de Callais: Released because of insufficient evidence.

92 December 1631: Jeanette Blanche: Not guilty of sorcery, but banished for want of respect for the court.

93 December 1631: Janette de Garis: As above.

94 December 1631: Susanne Molet: As above.

95 December 1631: Marie Clouet: As above.

96 January 1634: Jacob Gaudion of Alderney: Suspected, banished for ever.

97 May 1634: Marie Guillemette: Burnt at the stake.

98 May 1634: Emei Flères of Alderney: Burnt at the stake.

99 June 1639: Elizabeth Rolland: Burnt at the stake.

100 June 1639: Collette Sauvary: Burnt at the stake.

101 June 1639: Catherine Robert: Burnt at the stake.

102 June 1639: David de la Mare: Banished for seven years for 'lying habits'.

Pierre de Beauvoir, Bailiff

103 June 1644: Marie Robert: Result not recorded.

104 July 1649: Elizabeth L'Estasse: Suspected, banished for ever.

105 July 1649: Margueritte Preud'homme: Suspected, banished for ever.

JERSEY

Hostes Nicolle, Bailiff

1 1562: Michelle La Blance: Executed on the Vestue gibbet of Hures in St Ouen.

2 1562: Anne of St Brelade: Hanged.

3 May 1563: Thomasse Becquet: Acquitted.

George Paulet, Bailiff

4 1583: Marion Corbel: Died in Mont Orgueil before her trial.

5 November 1585: Jeanne Le Vésconte: Executed on the gibbet of Hures in St Ouen at the request of the Seigneur of St Ouen.

6 December 1585: Michielle Bellée: Hanged.

7 December 1585: Pasquette Le Vesconte: Executed after she had returned and resumed her 'malléces diabolicques'.

8 December 1585: Jean Morant: Hanged.

9 December 1585: Katherine Orenges: Hanged.

Jean Dumaresq, Bailiff

10 October 1591: Symon Vaudin: Hanged.

11 October 1591: Beneste Jamet: Hanged.

12 October 1591: Katherine Bertram: Hanged.

13 December 1591: Michiel Alixandre: Hanged.

144 December 1591: Collis Alixandre: Acquitted. (son of Michiel)

15 May 1593: Marie Poret : Committed to Castle; fate unknown.

George Paulet, Bailiff

16 July 1597: Pernelle Fallu: Released with warning.

17 October 1597: Peronelle Chevalier: Strangled at the post after several appearances for similar alleged offences.

8 December 1597: Françoise Le Méstre: Released with a warning.

19 January 1599: Marie Alixandre: Hanged. (Widow of Michiel)

20 December 1599: Marie Le Four: Acquitted.

21 December 1599: Marie Anley: Committed to Castle.

22 May 1600: Collette Amy: Hanged.

23 May 1600: Jeanne Hotton: Hanged.

24 May 1600: Phillipine Picot: Hanged, strangled.

25 June 1602: Marguerite Le Rues: Executed in St Ouen.

26 October 1602: Marie Rogerez: Executed in St Ouen.
(wife of Jacques Le Breton)

27 December 1605: Pasquette Guillaume: Executed after having been warned several times.

28 June 1606: Elizabeth Grandin: Released with a warning.

29 June 1606: Marie Grandin: Released with a warning.

30 June 1606: Marguerite Le Quesne: Released with a warning.

31 June 1606: Katherine Maugier: Executed after a previous warning.

32 October 1608: Michielle Bellenger: Hanged.

33 October 1606: Andrée Tourgis: Arrested for sorcery.
In the course of her trial she admitted to killing her grand-daughter.
Executed.

34 October 1608: Jean Tourgis: Acquitted.

35 October 1608: Marie Tourgis: Acquitted, and placed in the care of Mrs Rychard Hulvet.

36 October 1608: Marguerite Nyvret: Released with a warning.

37 June 1609: Thomyne Le Dain: Hanged.

38 June 1609: Georgette Alixandre: Banished.

39 October 1611: Collette Horman: Hanged.

40 October 1611: Isycles Hardyne: Hanged.

41 October 1611: Germaine Royl: Hanged.

42 October 1611: Georgette Alixandre: Banished for a second time.

43 December 1611: Perrine Alixandre: Refused to accept trial by Enquete. Fate not known.

44 December 1612: Susanne Corbel: Refused to submit to Enquete. Confined to Castle, fate not known.

45 February 1613: Jeanne Tourgis: Banished after admitting associating with witches.

Jean Hérault, Bailiff

46 October 1618: Marie Tourgis: Hanged.

47 January 1625: Collis Lamy: Warned and discharged.

48 October 1625: Marie Filleul: Executed on the gibbet at Samarès.

49 October 1625: Edouard Locquet:Hanged.

50 October 1625: Jeanne Orenge: Hanged.

51 October 1625: Raff Orenge: Hanged.

Philippe de Carteret, Bailiff

52 October 1626: Michelle Cosnefrey of Nomandy: Banished.

53 October 1626: Jeanne Umfrey of Normandy (mother of Collis Amy): Banished.

54 October 1631: Marie Grin: Refused to plead; sent to Castle; fate unknown.

55 October 1631: Jeanne Grandin of St Martin: Hanged.

George de Carteret, Bailiff

56 June 1648: Elizabeth Grandin: Rearrested; warned; discharged.

57 June 1648: Marie Grandin: Warned; discharged. (Daughter of Elizabeth)

58 June 1648: Marie Grandin of Trinity: Hanged.

59 June 1648: Marie Esnouf: Hanged.

60 June 1648: Clement Le Cerf: Banished. (Son of Marie Esnouf)

61 June 1648: Thomasse Le Ruez: Fate unknown.

62 May 1649: Guillemette du Vaistain: Flogged and banished. (Mother of Thomasse Le Ruez)

63 May 1650: Jean Machon: Refused Enquete and banished.

Michel Lemprière, Bailiff

64 November 1656: Jean Le Riche: Died in Castle before trial.

65 January 1660: Marie Jean of St Ouen: Executed. (Wife of Jean Le Dain)

Philippe de Carteret, Bailiff

66 October 1661: Sarah Lucette of St Lawrence: Banished. (Wife of Pierre Trachie.)

SELECTED BIBLIOGRAPHY:

Philip Ahier, 'Stories of Jersey Seas, of Jersey Coasts, of Jersey Seamen': Société Jersiaise, 1955. Albertus Magnus, 'Marvelous Secrets of Albert the Great': Paris, 1495. G.R. Balleine, 'A Bibliographical Dictionary of Jersey': London, 1948. Balleine's 'History of Jersey': Letchworth, 1981. G. R. Balleine, 'Witch trials in Jersey': Bullétins, La Société Jersiaise, 1939. John Bowle, 'A History of Europe': London, 1979. Aubrey Burl, 'Rings of Stone': London, 1979. Jean Chevalier, 'Journal': Société Jersiaise, 1906. S. Carey Curtis, 'Trials for Witchcraft in Guernsey': Transactions La Société Guernsiaise, 1937. Marie de Garis, 'Folklore of Guernsey': Guernsey, 1975. 'Croyances et Traditions Populaires en Normandie' (ed. R. de Mons): Cerisy-la-Salle, 1983. A. J. Eagleston, 'The Channel Islands Under Tudor Government': Cambridge, 1949. Marija Gimbutas, 'The Gods and Goddesses of Old Europe, 7000-3500BC: London, 1974. S. A. Handford (trans.) 'The Conquest of Gaul' by Julius Caesar: London, 1951. C. Hannay (trans.) 'A History of Sweden', by Ingvar Andersson: London, 1955. Chadwick Hansen, 'Witchcraft at Salem', London, 1970. Francis Hitching, 'Earth Magic': London, 1976. Hans Holzer (ed.) 'Encyclopedia of Witchcraft and Demonology': London, 1974. Pennethorne Hughes, 'Witchcraft': London, 1972. T. D. Kendrick, 'The Druids': London, 1928. Francis King, 'Magic: The Western Tradition': London, 1975. John L'Amy, 'Jersey Folklore': La Société Jersiaise, 1927. Raoul Lempriere, 'Customs, Ceremonies and Traditions of the Channel Islands': London, 1976. L. James Marr, 'A History of the Bailiwick of Guernsey': London, 1982. Increase Mather, 'Two Plain and Practical Discourses': London, 1669. Sir Edgar McCulloch, 'Guernsey Folklore': London, 1903. M. A. Murray, 'The Witch-Cult in Western Europe': Oxford, 1921. Joan Paisnel, 'The Beast of Jersey': London, 1972. J. L. Pitts, 'Witchcraft and Devil Lore in the Channel Islands': Guernsey, 1886. H. R. Trevor-Roper, 'Religion, the Reformation and Social Change': London, 1967. Barbara Rosen (ed.), 'Witchcraft': London, 1969. Jeffrey B. Russell, 'A History of Witchcraft, Sorcerers, Heretics and Pagans': London, 1980. Ward Rutherford, 'The Untimely Silence': London, 1973. Sheila Savill, 'Encyclopaedia of Myths and Legends': London, 1977. Montague Summers (trans.), 'Malleus Maleficarum' by Jacob Sprenger and Heinrich Kramer: London, 1928.' The Tacitus Annals' (various). K Thomas: 'Religion and the Decline of Magic' (Penguin). Marion G. Turk, 'The Quiet Adventurers in North America': Detroit, 1983. Paul Turner (trans.), 'The Natural History of C. Plinius Secondus': London, 1962. John Warburton, 'A Treatise of the History, Laws and Customs of Guernsey': 1822, Guernsey.